THE
ULTIMATE
GUIDE
TO
GOOD
CLEAN
HUMOR

Bernard Brunsting

BARBOUR
PUBLISHING, INC.
Uhrichsville, Ohio

THE
ULTIMATE
GUIDE
TO
GOOD
CLEAN
HUMOR

© 2000 by Bernard Brunsting.

Illustrations by Peg Buschman.

ISBN 1-57748-730-3

Published by Barbour Publishing, Inc., P.O. Box 719, Uhrichsville, Ohio 44683
http://www.barbourbooks.com

ecpa Member of the
Evangelical Christian
Publishers Association

Printed in the United States of America.

Dedication

To Alice,
my bride and joy for 58 years

Contents

Introduction

Herman Melville, the author of the classic novel *Moby Dick,* has well said, "A good laugh is a mighty good thing and rather scarce a thing."

This collection of good clean humor is my attempt to make a "good laugh" a little less scarce. I've shared this material, with positive results, with audiences all over the world, and my hope now is that this book will brighten your day, contributing to the emotional well-being of whoever reads or hears these jokes.

Please join me in this prayer found inscribed on a cathedral wall:

Give me a sense of humor, Lord;
Give the grace to see a joke,
To get some happiness from life
And pass it on to other folk.

BERNARD BRUNSTING
Stuart, Florida

Actors

The actor was talented, but unknown. A few minor roles in commercials and Grade B films were encouraging to his ego, but the fact was he couldn't make his monthly rent payment.

"Don't you realize," he explained to his pragmatic landlord, "that within a year or two, my fans will be flocking to this address, just to view the apartment where such a great talent once lived?"

"I expect my rent in two days," said the landlord. "If I don't get paid, your fans are free to come around and view the apartment where you once lived."

☆ ☆ ☆

An actor once rose to accept an award. "Don't worry," he began. "I won't speak very long. This tuxedo is due back in half an hour."

Throngs of admirers collected around the handsome actor at a shopping mall.

"Is that a real mustache?" one child asked.

"No, not this one," he said. "I keep my real one at home on the dresser."

Adam and Eve

Because it wasn't good for Adam to be all by himself, the Lord came down for a visit. "Adam," he said, "I have a plan to make you a very happy man. I'm going to give you a companion who will fulfill your every need and desire. She will be loving, beautiful, and faithful. She will make you feel wonderful every day of your life."

Adam was stunned. "That sounds incredible!"

"I'm glad you like the idea, but it doesn't come cheap. It will cost you an arm and a leg."

"That's a pretty high price to pay," Adam said. "What can I get for a rib?"

☆ ☆ ☆

Remember the immortal words of Eve, who said, "Don't forget, I wear the plants in this family!"

A Conversation Between Adam and God:

Adam: Why did you make Eve's hair so silky and lovely?

God: So you would like her.

Adam: Why did you make her skin so soft and nice to touch?

God: So you would like her.

Adam: But what I really want to know is: Why did you make her so dumb?

God: So she would like you.

☆　☆　☆

A little boy opened the big, old family Bible. With fascination, he looked at the yellowed pages and graphic pictures. Then something fell out of the Bible. He picked it up and looked at it closely. It was an old leaf from a tree that someone had pressed between the pages of the Bible.

"Mom, look what I found," he said to his mother.

"What is it dear?" she asked.

With astonishment in his voice, he answered, "It's Adam's clothes."

☆　☆　☆

"Adam and Eve must have been extremely bored," a child told her parents, shaking her head.

"What makes you think that?" asked her father. "They lived in the Garden of Eden, which was a living paradise on earth."

"Yeah, but, like, they didn't have anybody to gossip about."

Aging

Two children were caught in mischief by their grand-mother. Fortunately for them, she chose not to punish the youngsters. "Remember," she mused, "I used to be young once, too."

"Gee, grandma," said one of the kids, wide-eyed. "You sure have an incredible memory!"

☆ ☆ ☆

Toward the end of his career, concert pianist Mischa Elman said, "When I made my debut as a teenager in Berlin, people said, 'Isn't he wonderful for his age?' Now they're beginning to say the same thing again."

☆ ☆ ☆

A barber commented snidely as he cut a customer's hair, "A few gray hairs, I see."

"I don't doubt it," the gentleman said. "Can you work a little faster?"

When reporters came to see Winston Churchill on his eighty-seventh birthday, one of the young newspapermen said, "I hope to wish you a happy birthday, sir, when you are one hundred." Churchill replied, "I don't see why not, young man. You look healthy enough."

☆ ☆ ☆

Three older ladies were discussing the travails of getting older.

One said, "Sometimes I catch myself in front of the refrigerator with a jar of mayonnaise in my hand, and I can't remember whether I was taking it out or putting it away."

The second lady said, "Yes, sometimes I find myself on the landing of the stairs, and I can't remember whether I was on my way up, or on my way down."

The third lady chimed in, "Well, I'm glad I don't have those problems—knock on wood." She rapped her knuckles on the table, then cocked her head and said, "That must be the door. I'll get it."

☆ ☆ ☆

Sam looked in the mirror one day and saw he looked old. He decided to do something about it. He got a face lift. He bought a sporty car. He went to the youth shop for his clothes. He started to hang out with younger people. Everything was going along fine, but then he died. "Why me?" he asked, "just when everything was so good?"

"Why, Sam," he was told, "we're sorry, but we didn't recognize you."

Someone asked Armand Hammer about his formula for growing so old and staying so active. He listed three or four oft-mentioned things. The reporter said he'd had an uncle who did all of those things but died when he was sixty. Hammer replied: "His problem was that he didn't do them long enough."

✩ ✩ ✩

An older man met and courted an older woman. He chose a bench in a lovely park to propose to her. In the old-fashioned style, he got on his knees in front of her and said, "I have two questions. First, will you marry me?"

"Yes, I will," she answered. "And what is your second question?"

The older gentleman replied, "Will you help me up?"

✩ ✩ ✩

I know I'm losing the war with age. But I refuse to surrender.

✩ ✩ ✩

Growing old is like a roll of toilet paper. The closer you get to the end, the faster it goes.

Agatha Christie was asked, "What is it like to be married to an anthropologist?"

"It's just wonderful," she answered. "The older I get, the more interested he becomes."

☆ ☆ ☆

People can be frisky at any age. A newspaper article told about the police being called in to help quell a riot at a home for the elderly. Three militant octogenarians were arrested after a scuffle in the lounge. Leaders of an activist group had seized control and were holding the matron hostage in a closet. One eighty-year-old told reporters the demonstration was staged to enforce demands that old folks be given a larger role in management. "We have a bunch of young whippersnappers running things here and we don't trust anybody under sixty-five," one said.

Another commented, "What's the sense of living long if some fifty-year-old kid is going to tell you what to do?"

☆ ☆ ☆

Resisting the amorous advances of a woman, an elderly man explained, "My parents would not let me engage in anything like that."

"Your parents?" she asked in bewilderment, wondering how they could possibly still be alive.

"Yes, my parents," he repeated. "Mother Nature and Father Time."

You know you're getting old when you stoop to tie your shoes and wonder what else you can do while you're down there.

☆ ☆ ☆

Classified ad in a newspaper: "Retired schoolteacher, sick of reading, 'riting and 'rithmetic. Is there an elderly gentleman out there who can help me find the playground before the bell rings?"

☆ ☆ ☆

An elderly lady was filling out the registration form at a doctor's office. After recording her address, she came to the line marked "Zip." After thinking for a moment, she wrote, "Not bad for my age!"

☆ ☆ ☆

Doctor: "I can't find anything the matter with you, but I have one suggestion—that you cut back on your love life."

Elderly Man: "Okay, Doc, but which half should I give up—thinking about it or talking about it?"

☆ ☆ ☆

"Dad, what's middle age?"

"That's when you lose all your growth at the top and do all your growing in the middle."

"The older my grandpa gets," a girl remarked to a friend, "the farther he had to walk to school when he was my age."

☆　☆　☆

Doctor: "I'm doing what I can, but I can't make you any younger."
Patient: "I'm not interested in getting younger. I just want to get older."

☆　☆　☆

There is a lot to be thankful for if you take the time to look for it. For example, I am sitting here thinking how nice it is that wrinkles don't hurt.

Airplanes

For $10, visitors to the county fair could ride in a barn-stormer's biplane. An aging farm couple who'd never traveled outside the county thought they might like to take the opportunity to fly for the first time. But they were more than a little afraid.

"Tell you what," the barnstormer offered, perceiving their nervousness. "You can ride together, and I'll charge you only $5. Just promise me you won't scream or try to tell me how to fly my plane."

They accepted his offer and proceeded with the thrill of their lives. Through a wild series of loops and rolls, the pilot never heard a sound from his backseat companions.

"Wow, Pop, you were just great!" shouted the pilot over his shoulder as he landed the plane. "I thought for sure you'd both holler when we made that nosedive."

"That wasn't so bad," yelled the farmer. "But I almost broke my promise a few minutes before that, when Edna fell out of the airplane."

A teenager approached an airline ticket desk at the Indianapolis airport to inquire about an afternoon flight to Seattle. Without explaining to him the different time zones—Seattle is three hours behind—the agent punched a few keys on the computer and announced, "You can catch a flight at 5:02 P.M. nonstop to Seattle. It arrives at 5:24."

The youth rubbed his chin. "The plane leaves here at 5:02, and gets to Seattle at 5:24?"

"Yes."

"Today?"

"That's correct. Would you like to purchase a ticket?"

"No, I think I'll walk over there and watch that plane take off one time."

☆ ☆ ☆

The first-time flier was not assured when the flight attendant cheerily pointed out that the passenger seat could be removed and used as a flotation device. "I'd much rather be sitting on a parachute," he remarked to the person next to him.

☆ ☆ ☆

The first-time flier was very nervous as he buckled his seatbelt before takeoff. He turned to the woman in the next seat and asked, "About how often do jetliners like this crash?"

She thought a moment and replied, "Usually only once."

A man edged his way down the aisle to what he thought was his row aboard a jetliner awaiting takeoff. He looked at his ticket, then at the gentleman sitting by the window, then back at his ticket, then back at the gentleman.

"I have 17-F," he stated, getting the other's attention. "I believe you're in my seat."

"No, I'm in 17-D. Says so right here." He took out his own ticket and showed it to the man in the aisle.

"Yes, but 17-D is the aisle seat. You see, the seating runs from side to side, A-B-C and then D-E-F. A and F are the window seats, and C and D are the aisle seats."

"Nonsense. I asked them for a window seat, so this must be it. Seat 17-D, Flight 501 to St. Louis."

"Oh. Then you're definitely out of place. All the seats going to St. Louis are in the middle."

☆　☆　☆

Navy jet pilot: "This is it! We're flying faster than the speed of sound!"
Copilot: "What?"

☆　☆　☆

A nervous passenger decided to spring for one of those on-the-spot, low-investment, high-benefits insurance policies at the airport before her plane departed. Then she had time for a quick lunch, so she stopped at a Chinese restaurant along the concourse. Her eyes widened when she read the fortune cookie: "Today's investment will pay big dividends!"

After watching a news account of an airline crash, a teenager was asking his mother about the "black box" that's so important to accident investigators.

"It contains a complete record of the plane's diagnostics right up to the instant of the crash," she explained.

"Why isn't it destroyed on impact?"

"Because it's encased in a very special alloy material, I'm sure."

"Then why can't they make the whole airplane out of that material?"

☆ ☆ ☆

A flight attendant was surprised to hear a loud burst of laughter from the cockpit. A few seconds later, there was another outburst. Then a third.

The attendant opened the door to see what was going on. "What's the joke?"

"Oh, it's nothing, really," said the pilot. "I just get tickled when I imagine what the warden's gonna say when he discovers I've escaped from prison."

☆ ☆ ☆

"Would you please bring me some cotton balls?" an airline pilot asked a flight attendant as the plane began its landing approach.

"The change in air pressure hurts your ears, huh?" guessed the attendant with an understanding smile.

"No. But the yelling and shrieking will, after I inform the passengers that our landing gear won't go down and we have to do a belly slide."

The flight to England was halfway across the Atlantic when the pilot came on the intercom with a casual message to the passengers: "You may have noticed a slight change in the sound of the engines. That's because we've had to shut down Engine 2 temporarily. There's no cause for concern; we have three more engines in fine condition. But there'll be a slight delay. Our expected time of arrival has been changed from 2:14 P.M. to 2:45 P.M. Sorry for any inconvenience that may cause."

An hour later the pilot was back on the intercom, chuckling softly. "Folks, this is the first time I've ever experienced this, and I never thought it would happen, but we seem to have lost power in Engine 4. No problem in terms of safety, but we'll have a further delay. We now expect to arrive at Heathrow International at 3:30 P.M."

And a little while later he was back at the mike, still trying to sound reassuring but with an edge to his voice. "You won't believe this, but Engine 1 seems to be on the blink and we've decided it's wise to shut it down. This is a weird situation, but not really alarming. We can easily finish the flight with one engine, although we'll be flying substantially slower. We now anticipate arriving around 4:25."

One passenger turned to another and mumbled, "If that last engine goes out, it'll be next Tuesday before we get to England."

Animals

Several buzzards had been circling all day, looking for a dead animal carcass to eat. As night approached, one wearily suggested to the others, "Let's just kill some small animal and eat it. If we don't, we'll all die of starvation."

"Buzzards can't do that," croaked a second.

"Says who?"

"I read it in the nature encyclopedia."

☆ ☆ ☆

Two vultures were in the desert eating a dead clown.

The first vulture asks the second vulture: "Does this taste funny to you?"

☆ ☆ ☆

Why do hummingbirds hum?

Because they don't know the words.

Two women sat on a park bench. One was immersed in the newspaper, the other admiring the beauty of the falling orange leaves, the cool October breeze, the squirrels chattering and a million birds singing. "Oh, this is so wonderful," she couldn't help remarking. "Don't you just love the music of the birds?"

The other turned to her with a questioning frown. "Couldn't hear what you said. Can't hear anything at all, with these obnoxious birds and squirrels making such a racket."

☆ ☆ ☆

"I've lost my place in the Jones household," lamented one cat to a neighbor cat.

"What happened?"

"The old man bought a laptop computer."

☆ ☆ ☆

"Dad, don't we get leather from cows?"

"That's right, son."

"Doesn't leather shrink when it gets wet?"

"Usually."

"Then what happens to cows when they stand outside in the rain?"

☆ ☆ ☆

A duck walks into a drugstore and buys some Chapstick.

The clerk says, "Will that be cash or charge?"

The duck replies, "Just put it on my bill."

Mother and Father Rabbit were talking about the children after they had been put to bed.

"Why was Junior so happy this evening?" asked Father Rabbit.

"Well," explained Mother Rabbit, "he had a marvelous time at school. He learned to multiply."

☆ ☆ ☆

Upon entering the little country store, the stranger noticed a sign saying DANGER! BEWARE OF DOG! posted on the glass door. Inside, he noticed a harmless old hound dog asleep on the floor beside the cash register.

"Is THAT the dog folks are supposed to beware of?" he asked the store manager.

"Yep, that's him," the manager replied.

The stranger couldn't help but be amused. "That certainly doesn't look like a dangerous dog to me. Why in the world would you post that sign?"

"Because," the owner replied, "before I posted the sign, people kept tripping over him."

☆ ☆ ☆

Why did the gum cross the road?
It was stuck to the chicken's foot.

☆ ☆ ☆

Why did the chicken cross the road?
To prove to the possum that it could be done!

What does a fifty-pound canary say?
"Here kitty, kitty, kitty!"

☆ ☆ ☆

How do you get down off an elephant?
You don't. You get down off a goose.

☆ ☆ ☆

A duck waddled into a country grocery store and asked the clerk, "Do you sell duck food?"

"Of course not," replied the clerk. "We sell groceries to humans, not ducks."

The next day, the duck returned and asked again, "Do you sell duck food?"

Annoyed, the clerk snapped, "No! No duck food."

When the duck returned the next day and posed the same question, the clerk threatened, "I've told you this is a grocery store for people, not birds. If you ever come back in here and ask me that stupid question again, I'm going to nail one of your webbed feet to the floor and laugh while you walk around in circles."

The next day the duck was back. "Do you sell nails?"

The clerk, miffed, replied, "Of course not. This is a grocery store, not a hardware store."

Upon which the duck asked, "Do you sell duck food?"

☆ ☆ ☆

Two snakes were camouflaged in the jungle, feeding on passing insects. One remarked to the other, "Time's sure fun when we're having flies."

An out-of-towner drove his car into a ditch in a desolated area. Luckily, a local farmer came to help with his big strong horse named Buddy. The farmer hitched Buddy up to the car and yelled, "Pull, Nellie, pull!"

Buddy didn't move.

Then the farmer hollered, "Pull, Buster, pull!"

Buddy didn't respond.

Once more the farmer commanded, "Pull, Coco, pull!"

Nothing.

Finally, the farmer nonchalantly said, "Pull, Buddy, pull!"

The big horse leaned into the traces and easily dragged the car out of the ditch.

The motorist was most appreciative, but very curious. He asked the farmer why he'd called his horse by the wrong name three times.

The farmer shrugged and said, "Old Buddy's blind, and if he thought he was the only one pulling, he wouldn't even try!"

✩ ✩ ✩

One day an out-of-work mime was visiting the zoo and attempted to earn some money as a street performer. Unfortuantely, as soon as he started to draw a crowd, the zoo keeper grabbed him and dragged him into his office. But instead of telling the mime not to perform on zoo property, the zoo keeper explained that the zoo's most popular attraction, a gorilla, had died suddenly and the keeper feared that attendance at the zoo would drop off. He offered the mime a job to dress up as the gorilla until they could get another one. The mime accepted.

The next morning, he put on the gorilla suit and entered the cage before the zoo opened. When the crowds began to gather, the mime discovered that he'd stumbled onto a great job. He could sleep all he wanted, play all day, and make fun of people—and he was drawing bigger crowds than he ever had as a mime.

Eventually, however, the crowds began to tire of him and he grew bored just swinging on the trees in his cage. He noticed that the people were paying more attention to the lion in the next cage. Not wanting to lose his status as the zoo's most popular attraction, he climbed to the top of his cage, crawled across the partition and dangled from the top of the lion's cage. Of course, this made the lion furious, but the crowd loved it.

Well, this went on for some time. The mime in the gorilla suit kept taunting the lion, the lion kept roaring, the crowds grew larger, and the mime's salary kept going up. Then, one terrible day, as he was dangling over the furious lion, the mime slipped and fell.

When he found himself face-to-face with the lion, the mime was terrified. The lion gathered itself and prepared to pounce. The mime was so scared that he began to run around and around the cage with the lion in hot pursuit. The crowd roared its approval.

Finally, the lion caught up to the gorilla and pounced. The mime found himself flat on his back looking up at the angry lion and began screaming, "Help, Help me!"

Just then, the lion put his massive paw over the mime's mouth and said, "Shut up, you idiot! Do you want to get us both fired?"

A busy butcher noticed a dog in his shop and shooed him away. Later, he noticed that the dog was back again. He started to chase away the dog again, but then he noticed that the dog had a note in his mouth. The butcher took the note and read it.

May I please have twelve sausages and a leg of lamb? it said.

The butcher looked at the dog again, and lo and behold, in the dog's mouth, there was a ten dollar bill. So the butcher took the money, put the sausages and lamb in a bag, and placed it in the dog's mouth.

The butcher was very impressed, and since it was closing time, he decided to follow the dog home.

The dog was walking down the street and came to a crossing. He put down the bag, jumped up and pressed the crossing button. Then he waited patiently, bag in mouth, for the light to change. Then he walked across the road, with the butcher following.

Next, the dog then came to a bus stop and started looking at the timetable. The butcher was in awe. The dog checked out the times, then sat down on the bench to wait for the bus.

When the bus arrived, the dog walked to the front of the bus, looked at the number, then went back to the bench.

Another bus came, and again the dog went to look at the number. This time it was the right bus, and he climbed aboard. The butcher, by now open-mouthed, followed him onto the bus.

The bus traveled through town and out to the suburbs. Eventually, the dog got up, moved to the front of the bus and, standing on his hind legs, pushed the button to stop the bus. The dog got off, the bag of meat still in his mouth, and the butcher still following.

They walked down the road until the dog reached a house with a white picket fence. Letting himself in through the gate, the dog walked up up the path, and dropped the groceries on the step. Then he walked back several paces, got a running start, and threw himself—*whap!*—against the door.

He went back down the path, took another run, and threw himself—*whap!*—against the door again!

When there was no answer at the door, the dog went back down the path, jumped up on a narrow wall, and walked along the perimeter of the garden. When he reached a window, he banged his head against it several times. Then he walked back, jumped off the wall, and waited at the door.

Just then, a man opened the door and began laying into the dog, really yelling at him. The butcher ran up and shouted, "What are you doing? This dog is a genius. He could be on TV, you know!"

The man in the doorway looked at the butcher and snapped, "Clever, my eye. This is the third time this week he's forgotten his key!"

Art

A critic scowled up and down the aisles of a modern art exhibit. He stopped before one particularly abstract work.

"What in the world is that supposed to be?" he wondered aloud.

"That," said the artist, who happened to be standing nearby, "is *supposed* to be the Great Wall of China at sundown."

"Then why isn't it?" snapped the critic.

☆ ☆ ☆

A guy nearly got away with stealing several paintings from the Louvre. However, after planning the crime, breaking in, evading security, getting out, and escaping with the goods, he was captured only two blocks away, when his van ran out of gas.

He was asked how he could mastermind such a crime and then make such a stupid mistake.

"I had no Monet to buy Degas to make Van Gogh."

Ever since Leonardo da Vinci finished painting the *Mona Lisa*, people have asked why she is smiling.

Here's the answer: After the portrait was completed, the model was overheard saying, "By the way, Leo, your zipper's down."

☆ ☆ ☆

There's an easy way to understand modern art. If it's hanging on a wall, it's a picture. If you can walk around it, it's probably a sculpture.

☆ ☆ ☆

"What do you think of my painting?" the artist asked the critic.

The critic considered the question for a moment, then said, "It could be worse."

"I resent that," fumed the artist.

"Okay, it couldn't be worse."

Attitudes

Mrs. Avondale was walking an interior designer through the mansion, discussing renovations. The professional had many fine suggestions, and Mrs. Avondale accepted them all with the sweep of a hand.

"I only demand one thing," she said, turning to the designer. "When my best friend Marguerite comes in here after we're finished, I want her to drop dead from envy."

☆ ☆ ☆

Four cowboys were gambling for high stakes in an Old West saloon. One spread out four kings and proclaimed haughtily, "Looks like I win."

"Nope," growled another. "You don't win."

"What've you got?" demanded the first cowboy, astonished.

"Pair o' jacks and a Colt .45."

The first gambler pounded the table angrily. "It just ain't right. You been havin' all the luck."

A plumber knocked on the door. The lady of the house opened it and looked at him, puzzled. The plumber said, "I came to fix the leak in the kitchen."

The lady said, "What leak?"

"Aren't you Mrs. Thomas?"

"No, I'm Mrs. Collins. We bought this house from the Thomases a year ago."

"How do you like that?" the plumber groused. "They call up with an emergency, and then they move!"

Automobiles

A woman waited at a garage as mechanics scoured her car engine, trying in vain to pinpoint the problem. At length, a parrot in a corner cage sang out, "It's the thermostat."

"We've already checked the thermostat," grumbled one of the mechanics.

"It's the fan belt," the parrot ventured.

"No problem with the fan belt," said the other mechanic.

"It's the heat pump," said the parrot.

"It's not the bloody heat pump!" shouted the first mechanic, exasperated.

The woman was astounded by this exchange. "I've never heard of a bird so intelligent," she said.

"He's completely worthless," countered the second mechanic. "He'll talk your ear off, but he doesn't know the first thing about car engines."

Two street people were being entertained watching a teenager try to park a car across the street. The space was ample, but the driver just couldn't maneuver the car into it. Traffic was jammed. Angry drivers honked, further flabbergasting the poor youth. It took a full five minutes before the car was in place.

"That," said one of the idlers, "is what you call paralyzed parking."

✮ ✮ ✮

"What part of the car causes the most accidents?"
"The nut behind the wheel!"

✮ ✮ ✮

A rich suburbanite had car trouble while on a mountain holiday. He coaxed his car into the yard of a rickety roadside filling station and called to the greasy, bearded attendant, "Have you had any experience with BMWs?"

"Buddy, if I could work on cars like that," the attendant replied, "I don't reckon I'd be workin' *here.*"

✮ ✮ ✮

"The earth is round," the teacher said, "which means the surface of the earth is gradually curved."

"That explains it!" shouted Marcia.

"Explains what?"

"That explains why Mom's car pulls to the right."

The high school kid loved fast cars, and was thrilled to land a summer job at the local Alfa Romeo repair shop. "Gee, Mr. Vespucci," he gushed, grabbing a wrench, "I can't wait to learn all the ins and outs of fixing up these babies."

Mr. Vespucci told him to put down his tools and listen up. "Kid, the first thing you gotta learn," the mechanic told him, "is how to open the hood, stand back, and shake your head very, very sadly."

Bulletin Bloopers

Here is a sampling of announcements culled from various church bulletins. All of the examples are authentic:

The ladies of the church have cast off clothing of every kind, and they can be seen in the church basement on Friday afternoon.

☆ ☆ ☆

On Sunday a special collection will be taken to defray the expense of the new carpet. All those wishing to do something on the carpet will please come forward and get a piece of paper.

☆ ☆ ☆

Irving Jones and Jessie Brown were married on October 24. So ends a friendship that began in school days.

Thursday at 5 P.M. there will be a meeting of the Little Mothers Club. All wishing to become little mothers will please meet with the minister in the study.

✫   ✫   ✫

The Rev. Hamilton spoke briefly, much to the delight of the audience.

The pastor will preach his farewell message, after which the choir will sing, "Break Forth Into Joy."

✫   ✫   ✫

The choir will meet at the Friesen home for fun and sinning.

✫   ✫   ✫

During the absence of our pastor, we enjoyed the rare privilege of hearing a good sermon when J. A. Watts supplied our pulpit.

✫   ✫   ✫

For those of you who have children and don't know it, we have a nursery downstairs.

✫   ✫   ✫

The Low Self-Esteem Support Group will meet Thursday from 7:00 to 8:30 P.M. Please use the back door.

This afternoon, there will be a meeting in the south and north end of the church. Children will be baptized at both ends.

☆ ☆ ☆

The third verse of "Blessed Assurance" will be sung without musical accomplishment.

☆ ☆ ☆

Next Sunday, Mrs. Walters will be soloist for the morning service. The pastor will then speak on "It's a Terrible Experience."

☆ ☆ ☆

Due to the rector's illness, Wednesday's healing services will be discontinued until further notice.

☆ ☆ ☆

Reverend Jarvis has spoken in the largest churches in America. To miss hearing him will be the chance of a lifetime!

☆ ☆ ☆

Barbara C. remains in the hospital and needs blood donors for more transfusions. She is also having trouble sleeping and requests tapes of Pastor Jack's sermons.

There is joy in heaven over one singer who repents.

☆　　☆　　☆

Thursday night—Potluck supper. Prayer and medication to follow.

☆　　☆　　☆

The Youth Choirs have been disbanded for the summer with the thanks of the entire congregation.

☆　　☆　　☆

Jesus compared the kingdom to a treasurer hidden in a field.

☆　　☆　　☆

Please bring your baked goofs for the Fall Sale.

☆　　☆　　☆

Miss Charlene M. sang "I Will Not Pass This Way Again," giving obvious pleasure to the congregation.

☆　　☆　　☆

Our missionary speaker is Bertha Blech from Africa. Come tonight and hear Bertha Belch all the way from Africa.

Bumper Stickers

Jonah: SAVE THE WHALES

☆ ☆ ☆

Uriah: TAKE A HITTITE TO LUNCH

☆ ☆ ☆

The Israelites: HONK IF YOU LOVE MOSES

☆ ☆ ☆

Cain: CELEBRATE NATIONAL BROTHERHOOD WEEK

☆ ☆ ☆

Lot: IF YOU CAN SEE SODOM, YOU'RE TOO CLOSE

Elijah: MY OTHER CHARIOT ROLLS

☆ ☆ ☆

Joshua: JERICHO MUST GO

☆ ☆ ☆

VOTE NO ON THE SECOND COMMANDMENT

☆ ☆ ☆

Goliath: SUPPORT THE BAN ON SLINGSHOTS

☆ ☆ ☆

Paul: GRACE HAPPENS

☆ ☆ ☆

Methuselah: BE KIND TO SENIOR CITIZENS

Business Ventures

Reaching the end of a job interview, the corporate recruiter asked the young engineer fresh out of school, "And what starting salary were you looking for?"

The graduate said, "In the neighborhood of $75,000 a year, depending on the benefits package."

The recruiter smiled and said, "Well, what would you say to a package of five weeks' vacation, fourteen paid holidays, full medical and dental coverage, a company matching-fund retirement plan up to fifty percent of salary, and a new company car every two years—say, a red Corvette?"

The young engineer sat up in his chair and exclaimed, "Wow! Are you kidding?"

To which the company recruiter replied, "Certainly. . . but you started it."

After many, many years in business, a man's company was going down the drain. Unable to turn things around, and growing increasingly despondent, he finally called an old friend for advice.

After listening to the man's woes, his friend said, "Take a beach chair and a Bible and go down to the edge of the ocean. Sit right at the water's edge and open the Bible in your lap. Let the wind riffle the pages for a while until the Bible stays open at a particular page. Then, read the first words your eyes fall on and they will tell you what to do."

The businessman did as he was told. He drove to the beach with his chair and his Bible and sat right at the water's edge. He opened the Bible and let the wind riffle the pages until it stopped on a particular page. He looked down at the Bible and read the first words he saw. Then he packed up his chair and his Bible and drove home.

Three months later, the businessman and his family came to visit the friend. The man was wearing an expensive Italian suit, his wife was all decked out with a full-length mink coat, and his girls were dressed in beautiful silk dresses. The businessman handed his friend a thick envelope full of money to thank him for his wonderful advice. The friend was delighted and asked the man what words in the Bible had brought this good fortune to him.

The businessman replied, "I did what you said, and the first words I saw when I looked down at my Bible were 'Chapter 11.'"

Dakota tribal wisdom says that when you discover you are riding a dead horse, the best strategy is to dismount. However, in business, we often try the following strategies first:

1. Buy a stronger whip.
2. Change riders.
3. Create a training session to increase our riding ability.
4. Change the standards and declare that "this horse is not dead."
5. Provide additional funding to increase the horse's performance.
6. Form a quality circle to find uses for dead horses.
7. Promote the dead horse to a management position.

✩ ✩ ✩

Herschel was a salesman. One day, as he was driving across the Mojave Desert he spotted what looked like a body by the side of the road. Herschel slammed on the brakes, ran over, and discovered a man who appeared to be on the brink of death. Taking the poor man into his arms, Herschel bent close so he could make out the man's parched whisper.

"Water. . .thirsty. . .water."

"Are you in luck!" cried Herschel exultantly. "Why in my carrying case, which I happen to have right here beside me, I have the finest collection of one hundred percent silk neckties to be found this side of the Las

Vegas Strip. Normally, thirty-five dollars, but for you, twenty-two dollars and fifty cents."

"Water. . .thirsty. . .water."

"I'll tell you what. Since you seem like such a nice guy, I'll make it two for thirty-five dollars. That's for a poly-silk blend, though."

"Water. . .thirsty. . .water."

"You drive a hard bargain." Herschel shook his head regretfully. "Okay, any tie you want for sixteen dollars and fifty cents—but I can't go any lower."

"Water. . .thirsty. . .water."

"What's that? Oh, it's water you want. Why didn't you say so?" Herschel's voice was fillled with reproach. "Well, you're in luck again. Just over that sand dune is a lovely resort; I used to vacation there myself. They'll have all the water you can drink." With that, Herschel got back in his car and drove away.

With the prospect of nearby water to spur him on, the man managed to stagger to the top of the sand dune, and sure enough, a neon sign announcing Le Club Aqua was visible not far away. The man summoned the last of his strength, crawled across the burning sand to the resort's entrance, and collapsed. "Water. . .thirsty. . . water," he croaked.

"Ah, you want water," said the doorman sympathetically. "Well, you're in luck, we have all kinds. We have mineral water, ice water, club soda, Perrier, seltzer. Only thing is, you need to have a tie on to get in."

Carpenters

A policeman watched suspiciously as a man stepped out of a van, holding his hands about two feet apart. The man hurried down the street; the policeman followed. At the entrance to a building supply store, the suspect—hands still apart—waited until a customer came through the door. He darted through the open door behind the other person, seemingly afraid to touch the door with either hand.

The officer quietly entered the store behind him, just in time to hear the stranger tell a clerk, "I need half a dozen two-by-fours cut exactly this long."

☆ ☆ ☆

At a building site, a load of suspended lumber broke from a hoist and fell to the ground, burying a carpenter. Before his shocked coworkers could get to him, he rose from the rubble, dusted his overalls and hollered at the crane operator, "You klutz! You made me bite my lip!"

A residential building contractor went to a lumber yard and told the stock clerk he needed a truckload of two-by-fours.

"How long?" asked the clerk.

"I'll need 'em about forty or fifty years, I guess."

☆ ☆ ☆

A foreman making the rounds of a building site suddenly noticed one of his laziest workers was absent—again. "Hey, where's Sparkman?" he shouted.

"You must've missed his funeral," said a co-worker. "He's been dead and buried more than a month."

☆ ☆ ☆

Dad was pounding furiously with a hammer on a back porch wood project. Dogs barked. Neighbors phoned to complain. Items hanging on the wall were rocked off their mounts.

His two children watched as the family's portable weather station crashed to the floor. One child turned to the other and asked, "Is this what the weatherman means when he says the barometer is falling?"

Childish Wisdom

"Never sass a teacher whose eyes and ears are twitching."

Andrew, age 9

✧ ✧ ✧

"Always wear a hat when feeding seagulls."   *Rocky, age 9*

✧ ✧ ✧

"Sleep in your clothes, so you'll be dressed in the morning."

Stephanie, age 8

✧ ✧ ✧

"Never bug a pregnant mom."   *Nicholas, age 11*

✧ ✧ ✧

"Don't ever be too full for dessert."   *Kelly, age 10*

"Never ask for anything that costs more than $5 when your parents are doing their taxes."   *Carol, age 9*

☆ ☆ ☆

"Don't flush the toilet when your dad's in the shower."
                                                   Lamar, age 10

☆ ☆ ☆

"When your dad is mad and asks you, "Do I look stupid?" don't answer him."   *Heather, age 16*

☆ ☆ ☆

"Never tell your mom her diet is not working."
                                                   Michael, age 14

☆ ☆ ☆

"Don't pick on your sister when she's holding a baseball bat."   *Joel, age 12*

☆ ☆ ☆

"When you get a bad grade in school, show it to your mom when she's on the phone."   *Alyesha, age 13*

☆ ☆ ☆

"Never try to baptize a cat."   *Laura, age 13*

"Never spit when you're on a roller coaster."

Scott, age 11

☆ ☆ ☆

"Never do pranks at a police station." *Sam, age 10*

☆ ☆ ☆

"Beware of cafeteria food when it looks like it's moving."

Rob, age 10

☆ ☆ ☆

"Remember you're never too old to hold your father's hand." *Molly, age 11*

☆ ☆ ☆

"Listen to your brain. It has lots of information."

Chelsey, age 7

☆ ☆ ☆

"Stay away from prunes." *Randy, age 9*

☆ ☆ ☆

"Never dare your little brother to paint the family car."

Phillip, age 13

"Forget the cake, go for the icing." *Cynthia, age 8*

☆　☆　☆

"Remember the two places you are always welcome:
church and Grandma's house." *Joanne, age 11*

☆　☆　☆

When you want something expensive, ask your grandparents." *Matthew, age 12*

☆　☆　☆

"Never tell your little brother that you're not going to do
what your mom told you to do." *Hank, age 12*

Children

Mandy came crying to her dad. Between sobs, she explained that she'd traded her pet kitten Jingles to the children at the refreshment stand down the street for a cold drink.

"I see," he said, knowingly. "And now you miss little Jingles, don't you?"

"No," she said, "but I'm still thirsty, and I don't have anything else to trade."

☆ ☆ ☆

Two mothers were comparing child-rearing notes. "I just can't seem to get my children's attention," said one. "They stay mesmerized in front of the TV set. I say things to them and call for them, and they're oblivious to every word."

"Try sitting in an easy chair and looking like you're relaxed," said the other. "That gets my children's attention, without fail."

Michelle: "My parents have dreadful memories."
Chris: "Can't remember everything, huh?"
Michelle: "Oh, no. That's the problem. They *do* remember everything."

✩　✩　✩

Five-year-old Kristin was showing a neighborhood friend around her house. Her friend had never seen bathroom scales before and was mystified by the dial.

"What is this?" the friend asked.

"I'm not really sure. It's some kind of machine that puts grown-ups in a terrible mood."

✩　✩　✩

A jolly department store Santa Claus took a small girl on his knee and asked, "Now tell me the first thing you plan to do Christmas morning."

She thought, scratched her head, and replied, "Wake up."

✩　✩　✩

A father was scolding his children because they spent most of their summer days watching television. "Don't you know that laziness is a trap? You'll never amount to anything if you fall into lazy habits. It's hard work that pays off."

The oldest child replied, "Maybe it'll pay off when we grow up. But for now, being lazy seems to pay off a lot better."

Father: "You never know what you can do until you
    try."
Son: "I guess you never know what you *can't* do until
    you try, either."

☆　☆　☆

After being punished for losing his temper, a little boy
ventured to ask his mother, "What's the difference
between my foul temper and your worn nerves?"

☆　☆　☆

A schoolteacher phoned the home of one of her students. The father answered.

"I just wanted to ask if there's anything I can do," the
teacher said compassionately.

"Er, I don't think so. I believe we have everything
under control."

"Well, Jessy told me yesterday she would need to
miss class today because her mother's dying."

There was a long silence. "So, I take it Jessy wasn't at
school today?" the father asked suspiciously.

"Of course not. I told her she could be excused."

The parents immediately confronted their daughter.
"You told your teacher I was dying!" the mother shouted.
"That was a terrible lie. You know I'm perfectly well.
Why, I was working all day, as usual, except for a quick
trip to the beauty shop."

"Yep," Jessy said sweetly. "You were going to have
your hair dyed. That's basically what I told the teacher."

The tradition in the farm family was that when one of the boys misbehaved, he got a switching. And to drive the point home, he was required to go outside and cut his own switch.

Thus, bad little Ernie was sent out the door to select his means of punishment. Gone for several minutes, he finally returned with no switch—but with a handful of rocks.

"I couldn't find a good switch for you, Pa," he said. "Why don't you just stone me?"

☆ ☆ ☆

A little boy took the chair at the barber shop.

"How would you like your hair cut today, son?" asked the barber.

"Oh, do it like you do Daddy's, with the big hole at the back."

☆ ☆ ☆

"How far away is the sun?" a child asked her father.

"I'm not sure, honey."

"Well, how far away is the moon?"

"I don't know that, either."

"Do you know when the next solar eclipse will be?"

"Nope. Sorry."

"That's okay. Hope you don't mind me asking so many questions."

"Not at all. Asking questions is the only way to learn anything."

"I've never seen a hand so filthy," Mother said to Sammy when he came in from playing.

"Then take a look at this one," said Sammy, holding up his other hand.

✩　✩　✩

An eighth-grader was visibly frustrated as he struggled with his homework. Finally, he slammed the textbook shut, threw down his pencil and announced to his parents, "I've decided I'm a conscientious objector."

"Why did you decide that?" his father asked.

"Because wars create too much history."

✩　✩　✩

Micki's parents received a disturbing note from her second-grade teacher:

"Micki is an excellent student," the teacher began, "but when we have art and coloring projects, she draws everything in dark blue. Sky, grass, flowers, people, houses, kittens, cars, buildings, sun, moon, trees—all dark blue. This is unusual for a second-grader. Can you think of any explanation? If she's having some sort of emotional problem, we need to get to the bottom of it."

That night, the parents sat down with Micki and asked her why all her pictures were rendered in dark blue. "Why was that such a special color to her?" they asked.

"Well," she began, "I wasn't going to tell you. But see, about two weeks ago I lost my box of crayons. The only one left is the dark blue one I found in the front compartment of my book sack. . . ."

Six-year-old Alison was riding in the car with her mother. Mom tripped the turn-signal lever and prepared to make a turn. Alison was annoyed by the clicking sound emitted from the dashboard.

"Mom, why in the world did you turn that thing on?"

"To let other drivers know that I'm going to turn, dear."

"But Mom, nobody can hear it but you and me."

☆ ☆ ☆

Carolyn: "Mom, will you give me enough money to buy three cartons of milk?"

Mother, suspiciously: "Why do you want to buy three cartons of milk? We have milk in the refrigerator."

Carolyn: "Well, I don't really want to buy three cartons of milk."

Mother: "Then why did you ask for that much money?"

Carolyn: "Because with that much money, I could buy the new doll they have at the toy store."

☆ ☆ ☆

The mother was furious. "Ricky," she called to her son, "last night when I turned out the kitchen light and went to bed, there were four Twinkie packages in the cookie jar. This morning there are only two. What do you know about this?"

"Well, it was kinda dark," Ricky confessed. "I only saw two packages."

Two children were shouting at each other and were at the point of blows when Mom entered the playroom. "You two are always arguing," she scolded. "You need to learn to agree on things."

"We do agree," said one.

"Yeah," snarled the other. "We both agree we want the box of crayons *right now*."

☆　☆　☆

"Owww!" screamed six-year-old Cindy.

"What is it?" her mother called from the kitchen.

"The baby pulled my hair."

Mother came in to comfort Cindy. "Don't be angry at the baby," she said. "He doesn't understand that it hurts when he pulls your hair."

She'd no sooner returned to the kitchen when there came another shriek, this time from the toddler. Returning to the playroom, she was confronted by Cindy, who explained, "Now he understands."

☆　☆　☆

A child was thoroughly bored after being stuck inside the house all day because of rain. "Mom," she whined, "why does God send the rain, anyway?"

"To nourish the earth," her mother said. "That's how the crops and the flowers and the trees grow."

"But why does He make it rain in the parking lot where I like to go skating?"

A small child was working up the courage to confront the neighborhood bully. "Bullies are really wimps," he told himself as he rounded a fence corner. "Show me a bully, and I'll show you a real wimp."

To his horror, there stood the bully.

"Show you a bully, huh?" the mean boy said, sneering. "Well, you're looking at one."

The little boy screwed up his face and barked fiercely, "Yeah? And I'm showing you a real wimp!"

☆　☆　☆

Grandaunt Sarah, in town for a visit, was enjoying a glass of iced tea and having the most wonderful time talking with five-year-old Anne. "And have you been minding your table manners?" she asked.

"Oh, yes, ma'am. Mommy has taught me all the rules, and I follow them whenever I can."

"What are some of the rules you've learned, my dear?"

"Well, like, don't spit in other people's iced tea glasses."

☆　☆　☆

For weeks, a six-year-old boy kept telling his teacher about the baby that was expected at his house. One day, his mother let the boy feel the movements of the unborn child. He made no comment and stopped talking about it to his teacher. When the teacher asked him about the expected event, the boy burst into tears and said, "I think Mommy ate it."

Thad: "Mom, I sure wish I had a new skateboard like Jerry's."

Mother: "You shouldn't spend your life wanting things that other people have."

Thad: "But what other kinds of things are there to want?"

✩ ✩ ✩

"But why can't I talk inside the library?" Mandy asked her mother.

"Because you have to be quiet. Noise is a distraction. The people around you can't read."

"Can't read? Then why are they at the library?"

✩ ✩ ✩

Ideas children expressed:

Noah's wife was called Joan of Ark.

The fifth commandment is humor thy father and mother.

Lot's wife was a pillar of salt by day, but a ball of fire at night.

Christians can have only one wife. That's called monotony.

The pope lives in a vacuum.

A republican is a sinner mentioned in the Bible.

It is sometimes difficult to hear in church because the agnostics are so bad.

Kids in a Sunday school class had these definitions:

Adultery: The sin of saying you're older than you really are.

Conversion: The point after a touchdown.

Fast Days: The days you have to eat in a hurry.

Epistle: The wife of an apostle.

☆ ☆ ☆

A mother came home from shopping and found her freshly baked pie dug out crudely from the center. A gooey spoon lay in the sink and crumbs were scattered over the kitchen counter and floor.

She called her son into the kitchen. "Peter," she said sternly, "you promised me you wouldn't touch that pie before dinner."

Peter hung his head.

"And I promised you I'd spank you if you did," she continued.

Peter brightened. "Now that I've broken my promise," he offered, "it's OK with me if you break yours, too!"

Churches

Two children were among the worshipers filing into the sanctuary on the first Sunday morning in January. One frowned and pointed to the Christmas tree, which still stood in honor of the Advent season. "Why is the Christmas tree still up?"

"Because it isn't December 25 yet," the other child answered.

☆ ☆ ☆

The clerk of the church board continually opposed the pastor's proposal to get a chandelier for the church. Finally, the pastor took him aside and asked him why he always blocked his proposal. The clerk told him, "Pastor, I have three good reasons. In the first place, I don't know how to spell it for the minutes. In the second place, we haven't got anyone in the church who can play one of those things. And, third, what we really need is a new light fixture for the sanctuary."

A minister was reading the minutes of a board meeting he had missed because of illness. His heart was warmed when he read, "A motion was made to pray for the recovery of the minister." But the next sentence put everything in perspective: "The motion passed, by a vote of seven to five."

☆ ☆ ☆

A family who'd just moved into town spent Sunday mornings for the first few months visiting different churches. Returning home after one service, the eight-year-old remarked, "We definitely don't wanna join that church."

"Why not?" asked Dad.

"This is the third time we've been there, and it's rained every time."

☆ ☆ ☆

The congregation sang "The Star Spangled Banner" one Sunday. As soon as it was finished, a young boy yelled out, "Play ball!"

☆ ☆ ☆

One child's version of John 3:16: "For God so loved the world that He gave His only begotten Son, that whoso-ever believeth in Him should not perish, but have ever-laughing life."

"Pastor, do you believe in ghosts?"

"No—not in the popular sense, at any rate. Why do you ask?"

"We're considering buying the old Carter mansion on South Main Street. It's a beautiful Victorian, and we'd love to restore it. But everyone says it's haunted by the ghost of old Mr. Carter."

"Well, my opinion is that if his soul's in hell, he can't return. If he's in heaven, he doesn't want to."

☆　☆　☆

Over the massive front doors of a church, these words were inscribed: THE GATE OF HEAVEN. Below was a small sign: PLEASE USE OTHER ENTRANCE.

☆　☆　☆

"If no one said anything unless he knew what he was talking about," an exasperated moderator said at a raucous church meeting, "a ghastly hush would descend upon this place."

☆　☆　☆

"King David used to be a hero of mine, but not anymore," little Brodie told his mother after church one Sunday.

"Why not, son?"

"I learned today that he killed the Jolly Green Giant."

A pastor said to a member of his church, "I wish I had ten members just like you."

"It's good to hear you talk like that," the parishioner replied, "but I am surprised. You know that I complain about a lot of things around here. I often tell you I thought your sermon was dreadful, and I hardly give anything. Why would you want ten people like me?"

"Like I said, I wish I had ten members just like you. The problem is, I have fifty like you."

☆ ☆ ☆

A country church held a covered dish supper on opening night of its revival series. The guest preacher was invited to lead the food line, but he declined. "I can't eat a big meal before I preach," he explained to the congregation. "It detracts from my ability to deliver a good sermon."

Two hours later, several women were cleaning up the church kitchen. "I declare," mumbled one, "I believe that preacher might as well have eaten his fill at suppertime."

☆ ☆ ☆

An older gentleman had a parcel weighed for shipment at the post office.

"Are any of the contents breakable?" asked the clerk.

"Depends on who you are, I suppose."

"What do you mean?"

"There's an antique Bible in that package. To me, the Ten Commandments are unbreakable. I can't speak for you, though."

A minister got hold of a way to make his church friend-
lier when he visited another church where they followed

the practice of greeting
each other during
the worship service.
He told his congre-
gation about it and
said it would be
included in the
program the next
Sunday. But one
man got so enthusi-
astic about the idea
that he grabbed the hand of a lady behind him and
greeted her. She gave him an icy stare and told him,
"That friendliness business doesn't start until next week."

☆ ☆ ☆

"I love it when we sing hymns I've never heard before."

☆ ☆ ☆

Little Rodney seemed troubled at Sunday dinner. "What
is it, son?" his dad asked.

"I really didn't like that violent hymn we sang in
church," Rodney said.

"Violent? What hymn was violent?"

"You know. The one that goes, 'There is a bomb in
Gilead.'"

A church is an excellent place to go for faithlifts.

☆　☆　☆

"Dad, are people really made of dust, like the Bible says?"

"In a sense, yes."

"And we're all going to return to dust when our bodies die?"

"Certainly. Why do you ask?"

"Well, I was looking under my bed and I saw somebody either coming or going."

☆　☆　☆

SOME THINGS YOU'VE PROBABLY NEVER HEARD IN CHURCH:

"Hey! It's our turn to sit on the front pew!"

"I was so enthralled, I never noticed your sermon went for forty-five minutes."

"Personally, I find witnessing much more enjoyable than golf."

"I'm tired of doing it the old way. Let's try something new."

Church Signs

Free trip to heaven. Details inside!

✮ ✮ ✮

Try our Sundays. They are better than Baskin-Robbins.

✮ ✮ ✮

Searching for a new look? Have your faith lifted here.

✮ ✮ ✮

Having trouble sleeping? We have sermons—come hear one!

✮ ✮ ✮

When down in the mouth, remember Jonah.
He came out all right.

God so loved the world that he did not send a committee.

☆ ☆ ☆

Come in and pray today. Beat the Christmas rush!

☆ ☆ ☆

Sign broken. Message inside this Sunday.

☆ ☆ ☆

Fight truth decay—brush up on God's Word daily.

☆ ☆ ☆

How will you spend eternity?
Smoking or Non-smoking?

☆ ☆ ☆

The minimum wage just went up, but the wages of sin stayed the same.

☆ ☆ ☆

If you're headed in the wrong direction,
God allows U-turns.

☆ ☆ ☆

Do not wait for the hearse to take you to church.

If you don't like the way you were born,
try being born again.

☆ ☆ ☆

Forbidden fruit creates many jams.

☆ ☆ ☆

In the dark? Follow the Son.

☆ ☆ ☆

Running low on faith? Stop in for a fill-up.

☆ ☆ ☆

If you can't sleep, don't count sheep.
Talk to the Shepherd.

Clergy

One boy, whose father was a salesman, was bragging that all his father had to do was sell a car and he made fifty dollars. A second boy, whose father was a lawyer, said, "That's nothing. My father merely gives advice and he collects five hundred dollars." The third boy, whose father was a minister, was not to be outdone and he boasted, "My father gives a talk, and it takes eight men to bring him his money."

☆ ☆ ☆

A minister's wife was in the habit of signaling her husband during sermons to let him know how the message was going. A little wave of the hand over the head indicated that the message was going over their heads; a cupped ear meant he should speak up; a slash across the throat told him it was time to quit. One day he got carried away in his sermon and forgot to look in her direction for a while; when he did, he found her pinching her nose between her thumb and forefinger.

Some men went to pick up the visiting minister, whom they had never met, from the station. Going up to one man getting off the train, they asked him if he was the guest minister. "No," he told them. "It's my ulcer that makes me look like this."

☆ ☆ ☆

A minister, who had been knocked off a motorbike while on vacation in Bermuda, was trying to explain to his congregation why his leg was in a cast. One parishioner cut short his story by saying, "It could have been worse."

"How could it be worse?" the pastor protested. "I broke my leg in two places, the ligaments are ruptured, my ankle was dislocated, and I have to be in a cast for three months. I even have to sit on a bar stool to preach. How could it be worse?"

"You could have broken your jaw."

☆ ☆ ☆

The Perfect Pastor never forgets a name. He smiles all the time with a serious face. He is thirty-eight years old, with forty years' experience. If your pastor doesn't measure up, simply send this letter to six other churches who are tired of their pastor, too. Then bundle up your pastor and send him to the church at the top of the list. In three weeks you will get 634 pastors, one of whom should be perfect. Have faith in this letter. One church broke the chain and in less than three months got its old pastor back again.

Torrential rains were swiftly flooding the town's streets. A preacher sat on his porch watching the deluge. As the rising water approached his front steps, a rescue squad boat motored by. "Come aboard, Preacher!" shouted one of the officials. "We'll carry you to safety."

"I'm safe enough," the preacher replied. "I'm trusting the Lord to protect me and my home."

Half an hour later, the water was up to the porch floor. Another boat glided past. "Jump aboard, Preacher! It's going to get worse!"

"I'm not afraid, friends. The Lord will deliver me from drowning."

Late in the day, the flood had almost engulfed the town's buildings. The preacher was on the roof, clinging to the chimney, when a helicopter hovered overhead. A rope was cranked down—and astonishingly, the preacher waved the crew away. "The Lord Himself will save me," he declared.

And as darkness descended, the preacher was swept to his death.

The next thing he knew, he was at heaven's gate, waiting at the desk of St. Peter. The venerable saint looked up from his writing. "You!" he exclaimed. "What are you doing here already?"

"Well," the preacher stammered, "I was down there in the flood, waiting for the Lord to rescue me, and finally the water just got too high and. . ."

"Saints, man! We sent you two boats and a helicopter!"

A rabbi and a pastor were at a neighborhood picnic in a nearby park. As they rode in a boat out on the lake, the rabbi stood up, stepped out, and walked over the water to the nearest stretch of land.

Astonished, the minister decided to see if he could duplicate this miraculous feat. He stepped out of the boat—and immediately went under. After he'd managed to swim ashore and was drying himself off, the rabbi walked over and said, "Next time I'll show you where the rocks are!"

☆ ☆ ☆

A mother came into her son's room to get him up for church. He didn't want to go. He said, "I don't like the way they sing the hymns. The choir is awful. The sermons are dull. I just don't want to go."

"But you must go," she told her son. "After all, you are the minister."

☆ ☆ ☆

The pastor felt sorry for the old man he saw in the park every morning as he walked to the church. It seemed the world had been hard for him. One morning, he handed the man an envelope with $10 inside and a note, "Never Despair." The next day the man handed him $60 in return. "What's this for?" the astonished minister asked.

"Never Despair was in the money in the second race," the man replied.

"I'm sorry about the delay, Reverend," the passport officer said. "Everyone waits until the last moment to get ready for a trip they know they are going to take."

"I understand," the minister said. "I have the same problem in my business."

☆ ☆ ☆

The new minister came to his office the first morning of his new assignment. He found three envelopes on his desk from the previous pastor.

The first was marked, "Open if you run into trouble."

On the second was the note, "Open if you run into bad trouble."

The third: "Open if the trouble is disastrous."

There was no need to open any envelope for quite some time. But the honeymoon finally ended and the time came when he found he was having difficulty. It was enough to make him remember the envelopes which he had put away in a drawer. He opened the first envelope and found the suggestion: "Blame your predecessor." He took the advice and it seemed to work—at least for a while.

Things went along fine for quite some time and then trouble, more serious this time, struck. It was time for the second envelope—which he quickly opened. This time he read, "Blame the denomination." Again he found relief. He was grateful for the letters.

A few years later, the trouble was really bad. Once more, he resorted to the helpful words of his predecessor. The message in the third envelope read, "Prepare three envelopes."

A minister asked his wife, "How many great preachers do you think there are in the country?"

"Well, I really don't know," she answered sweetly, "but probably one less than you think."

☆ ☆ ☆

The U.S. Patent Office once required inventors to send a model of their inventions along with their patent applications. An accumulation of these was then auctioned off. One was an anti-snoring device: a rubber tube connected the mouth with the ear so a snoring person would wake himself up. Another was a device whereby a mother could rock her baby and churn butter at the same time. Another was a pulpit that majestically rose from beneath the floor. "One day," the auctioneer said, "the minister was flailing away at the sins of the world from his state-of-the-art pulpit. His subject was, 'Where will you spend eternity?' Just after asking that question, he hit the wrong button and disappeared out of sight."

☆ ☆ ☆

A pastor was trying to negotiate a lower price for his auto repairs. "Remember," he pleaded, "I'm a poor preacher."

"I know," the mechanic replied. "I was in church on Sunday."

A well-meaning, but fumbling Welsh preacher had never been out of his small parish or away from the local language. To overcome his parochialism, he decided to take a trip to New York. One of his parishioners asked him to look up her son in the big city and find out why he never wrote to his mom. His name was John Dun.

After arriving in New York, the man of the cloth was walking down a street and saw a sign in a window: "Dun and Bradstreet."

"Ah," he thought, "this must be it." He walked in and in halting English asked the girl at the reception desk, "Where's John?" She told him, "Down the hall and the third door on the left."

Just as he was about to open the third door on the left, a man came out and the minister asked him, "Are you Dun?"

The man, a bit jarred by the strange question, replied, "Yes, I'm done."

"Then," said our friend from Wales, "Why don't you write your mother?"

☆ ☆ ☆

Two pastors were discussing their respective churches.

"How big of a church do you have?" the minister of the smaller church was asked.

After hearing his answer, the other pastor proceeded to brag about his big congregation.

When he had finished, the pastor of the little church said, "Well, I never wanted to be a great preacher, and it's working out really well."

Lost on his way to speak at a church, Bishop Fulton Sheen asked a little boy to help him find it. The little boy asked him why he was going to the church. "To speak," Sheen told him.

"What about?" the boy wanted to know.

"I'm going to tell people how to get to heaven," he replied.

The little boy laughed and when the bishop asked him what was so funny, said: "You're going to tell them how to get to heaven when you can't even find the church."

A minister tried to console a parishioner who seemed crestfallen because the pastor was leaving. "You'll get a good new minister," he reassured him.

The man replied, "That's what they told us the last time."

College

A student studied very hard for a course on birds. On the day of the test, he was shocked when the teacher pulled out a chart of birds' legs. He couldn't believe that after all his hard work, he had not studied anything about legs. In his disgust, he got up to leave. "Just a moment," the teacher said. "What is your name?"

The student pulled up his pant legs and said, "Guess!"

☆ ☆ ☆

"I'll never finish that book report," moaned the English major. "It's due tomorrow, and I've read only two chapters."

"No sweat," said the roommate. "Those new literary briefs at the campus bookshop are great. Scan over them for twenty minutes, and half your work is done!"

"Gee, thanks! I'll buy two copies, then!"

A professor was turned down on his application to a new college post. "Not enough published work," said the dean. "You have only one book to your credit."

"Are you aware that God Himself has only one book to His credit?"

"Then He needn't apply here."

☆ ☆ ☆

A professor asked a student to remain for a few moments after class.

Holding out the young man's assignment, the professor asked, "Did you write this poem all by yourself?"

The student said, "Every word of it."

The professor stuck out his hand and said, "Well, then, I'm glad to meet you, Mr. Wordsworth. I thought you were long dead!"

☆ ☆ ☆

A woman was telling her friend about Christmas at her house: "I had a visit from a jolly man with a big bag over his shoulder."

☆ ☆ ☆

A college student in a philosophy class was taking his first exam. The test consisted of a single line, which simply read, "Is this a question? Discuss."

After a short time, he wrote, "If that is a question, then this is an answer."

The student received an A on the exam.

Father: "You're telling me your entire class got an A in philosophy? How?"
Daughter: "We proved the professor didn't exist. What could she do?"

☆　☆　☆

The parents of a first-year college student received this note from their child:

Dear Mom & Dad,
    Univer$ity life i$ $o wonderful! Cla$$e$ are intere$ting, cla$$mate$ are the be$t. The only thing I need right now i$ a little ca$h.
                                                    Love,
                                                    Dabney

After deliberating, they drafted an appropriate response:

Dear Dabney,
    NOt much is happening here on the NOrth side of town since you left for NOrthwestern U. See you at Thanksgiving in NOvember? Loved your letter. Write aNOther one when you have time. Have to go NOw.
                                                    Love,
                                                    Mom & Dad

It was the final examination for an introductory English course at the local university. Like many such freshman courses, it was designed to weed out the weaker students. The professor was very strict and told the class that any exam not on his desk in exactly two hours would not be accepted and the student would fail.

Thirty minutes into the exam, a student came rushing in and asked the professor for an exam booklet.

"You're not going to have time to finish this," the professor stated sarcastically as he handed the student a booklet.

"Yes I will," the student replied confidently. He then took a seat and began writing. After two hours, the professor called for the exams, and the students filed up and handed them in—all except the late student, who continued writing. A half-hour later, the late student came up to the professor, who was sitting at his desk preparing for his next class. He attempted to put his exam booklet on top of the stack that was already there.

"Oh no you don't," the professor warned. "I'm not going to accept that. It's late." The student looked incredulous and angry. "Do you know WHO I am?" he snapped.

"No, as a matter of fact I don't," replied the professor with an air of sarcasm in his voice.

"DO YOU KNOW WHO I AM?" the student asked again, raising his voice even louder.

"No, and I don't care," replied the professor with an air of superiority.

"Good," replied the student as he quickly lifted the stack of completed exams, stuffed his in the middle, and walked out of the room.

A linguistics professor was lecturing to his class one day. "In English," he said, "a double negative forms a positive. In some languages, though, such as Russian, a double negative is still a negative. However," he pointed out, "there is no language wherein a double positive can form a negative.

A voice from the back of the room piped up, "Yeah. Right."

Computers

Two information services managers were complaining about their work.

"If our computers could think for themselves, my problems would be over," said one.

"If my technical staff could think for themselves, so would mine," said the other.

☆ ☆ ☆

While trying to run four different programs in memory and juggle data between them, a typist saw this error message appear onscreen: FORGET IT. YOU'RE ASKING TOO MUCH.

☆ ☆ ☆

Another computer operator received this error message: THREE THINGS IN LIFE ARE GUARANTEED: TAXES, DEATH, AND COMPUTER CRASHES. GUESS WHICH ONE JUST HAPPENED?

What's the first symptom of a computer that's getting old?

Memory problems.

☆ ☆ ☆

A repairman came in to fix the new, giant supercomputer. After studying it for a moment, he took out a screwdriver and turned a small screw an eighth of an inch counter-clockwise. The computer started to hum. The repairman filled out a bill for three hundred dollars and handed it to the company accountant. The accountant considered that three hundred dollars was a bit much for such a simple repair and demanded that the bill be itemized.

Taking the invoice back from the accountant, the repairman wrote:

Turning screw one-eighth of an inch: $.50
Knowing where to turn: $299.50

☆ ☆ ☆

A sales clerk in an electronics store noticed a customer staring at a display unit. The display was a voice-activated computer with a built-in-microphone.

The clerk sauntered over and whispered to the baffled customer, "It's a voice computer. You simply speak to it, as you would to a person. The first thing it needs to know, in order to begin operating, is your name."

The customer watched the clerk walk away, then leaned near the computer and whispered, "My name's Sam Smith. What's your name?"

What's a tall computer's worst fear?
A slipped disk.

☆ ☆ ☆

A child was watching his mother sift through and delete a long list of junk E-mail on the computer screen.

"This reminds me of the Lord's Prayer," the child said.

"What do you mean?"

"You know. That part about 'deliver us from E-mail.'"

☆ ☆ ☆

"I'll just never be able to use computers," whined Grant. "I don't think I have the basic aptitude for them."

"But they're so easy to use these days," said Cameron. "A lot of times, the only thing you have to do to answer the computer's prompts is PRESS ANY KEY."

"Yeah, that's one of my problems. I've never been able to find the 'ANY' key."

Cowboys

Two aged wranglers were relaxing in the bunkhouse, yearning for the old times.

"I hate all this automobile traffic around here," one said. "There are too many cars and trucks on the road for safety, these days."

"Well, one good thing's come of it," said his partner.

"And just what, exactly, might that be?"

"Not nearly as many rustlers to track down."

☆ ☆ ☆

Dude: "What's the name of this ranch?"
Rancher: "Why, it's the Bar-B Double-D Crooked-T Circle-M."
Dude: "Kinda hard to remember all that, ain't it?"
Rancher: "I s'pose so."
Dude: "Where are all the cows?"
Rancher: "Can't keep any. One look at that branding iron, and they're *gone!*"

Why do cowboys need two spurs? Are they afraid one side of the horse might take off galloping by itself?

☆ ☆ ☆

A tough old cowboy counseled his grandson that if he wanted to live a long life, the secret was to sprinkle a little gunpowder on his oatmeal every morning.

The grandson did this and lived to be ninety-three.

When he died, he left fourteen children, twenty-eight grandchildren, thirty-five great-grandchildren, and a fifteen-foot hole in the ceiling of the funeral home.

☆ ☆ ☆

A dusty cowboy rode into town, shuffled into the barbershop, sank into the barber's chair and said, "Gimme a shave, partner."

"That'll be a mite hard, with your head slumped so low," the barber observed.

The cowboy pondered a minute. "All right," he conceded. "Then gimme a haircut."

Crime and Punishment

Judge, to repeat offender: "What are you charged with this time, Mr. Smith?"

Smith: "I was just trying to get my Christmas shopping done early."

Police officer: "Yes—before the store opened, Your Honor."

☆ ☆ ☆

A man accused of murder felt a wave of panic as he surveyed the jury. Somehow he was able to contact one of the jurors and told her he would give her a big sum of money if she would hold out for manslaughter. The verdict came in—he was found guilty of manslaughter.

With tears of gratitude he asked her, "How did you do it?"

"It wasn't easy," she told him. "They all wanted to acquit you."

The governor was visiting the state penitentiary and chatting with a few of the inmates as he walked down a corridor of cells.

"What are you here for?" he asked one prisoner.

"I was framed. They convicted me of embezzlement, but it was my business partner who plotted the whole thing and got all the money."

"And what about you?" he asked another.

"Armed robbery—but it was a case of mistaken identity. Some of the witnesses picked me out of a lineup, but I swear the real robber was somebody who just happened to look like me."

One by one, the inmates he spoke to declared their innocence—until he came to the last man on the cell block. "Perjury," the man answered. "I did it, sure enough. I made a terrible mistake, and now I'm paying for it, fair and square."

The governor turned to the warden and ordered the man released immediately.

"But why?" the warden asked, amazed.

"Because he's a crook," the governor said loudly. "He admits it. He's a bad example, contaminating the minds of this whole block of innocent men, and he needs to be removed."

☆　☆　☆

A prisoner fell in love with the warden's daughter and married her. The warden was miserable—it seems they'd eloped!

Several security guards were scratching their heads in the aftermath of a bank robbery.

"But how could they have gotten away?" one wondered aloud. "We had all the exits guarded."

"I think they must have gone out the entrance," suggested another.

✩ ✩ ✩

Judge: Have you anything to offer this court before I pass sentence?
Defendant: Nope. My lawyer took every last penny.

✩ ✩ ✩

It was the annual baseball game between the townspeople and the inmates at the local prison. When his turn at bat came up, the leading hitter of the prison team took a vicious swing and sent the ball zooming into the far reaches of the outfield. He rounded first. He rounded second. He rounded third and headed for home. They finally caught him between third base and the Mexican border.

✩ ✩ ✩

A young man ran afoul of the law out west and was hanged for his crime. The sheriff, wanting to break the news to the family as gently as he could, wrote: "I regret to inform you that your son died here recently while taking part in a public ceremony. The platform on which he was standing gave way, and his neck was broken when he fell."

The kindergarten class went on a field trip to the local police station where an officer showed them around. Stopping in front of a Ten Most Wanted poster, he explained how citizens often helped bring about arrests.

"Are those pictures of the bad guys?" asked one six-year-old.

"Yep, those are the bad guys," the policeman confirmed.

"Well," pursued the youngster, "why didn't you hold on to them when you took their pictures?"

☆ ☆ ☆

A poor bookseller walked through Central Park on his way home each evening. One Monday, a masked man jumped from behind a tree. "Give me your money!"

"I have no money. I'm just a poor bookseller. Here's my wallet; see for yourself."

Finding the wallet and the victim's pockets all empty, the bandit grumbled and ran off.

The next Monday, the same bandit accosted the bookseller. "Give me your money!" Again, he made off without a dime.

This happened each Monday evening for a month. Finally, the bookseller said to him, "Look, you recognize me. You know I'm only a poor bookseller and I don't carry any money at all. Why do you waste your time and risk getting caught every Monday?"

The robber replied, "I'm still practicing, and you don't seem to mind too much."

"That'll be ten years," the judge announced harshly at the conclusion of a robbery trial. "Does the defendant have anything more to say to the court?"

"Your Honor," the defendant pleaded, "there's no way I could've been the guy who robbed that bank. I swear I was all the way across town holding up a convenience store at exactly the same moment the bank was being heisted."

"Make that twenty years," said the judge.

✧ ✧ ✧

After weeks of agonizing physical training, police academy cadets still hadn't been admitted to the firing range.

"I don't get it," huffed one trainee to another as they pounded out yet another five-mile jog.

"What do you mean?"

"We still don't know how to protect people and property, but we're getting real good at running away."

✧ ✧ ✧

The first morning of a general sessions court term brought scores of defendants, police officers, prospective jurors, and lawyers into the courtroom. The hubbub was so impossible that the presiding judge cracked her gavel. "I'll throw out the next person who makes a sound!"

To which a chorus of criminals and their defense lawyers roared, "Hurrah!"

A new prisoner was shown to a cell he was to share with a crusty old crook.

"How long is your sentence?" was the veteran's first question.

"Well, thirty years—but I'm up for parole in ten," said the rookie.

"Then I get the bunk nearest the door," said the vet. "My parole comes up in only six years."

☆ ☆ ☆

Judge: "You're accused of stealing a typewriter. How do you plead?"

Defendant: "I'm innocent, Your Honor. That whole thing was a mistake."

Judge: "How so?"

Defendant: "I thought it was the cash register."

☆ ☆ ☆

"The prosecutor says she can produce five witnesses who saw you running from the bank with the money bags," a defense lawyer confided to a suspect.

"That's nothing," said the suspect. "I can produce 500 witnesses who didn't see me running from the bank."

Critical Thinking

If you find any mistakes in this book, they are there for a purpose. We try to offer something for everyone. Some people always look for mistakes, and we don't want to disappoint them.

☆ ☆ ☆

In a *Peanuts* cartoon, Linus asks Lucy, "Why are you always so anxious to criticize me?"

Her response was typical of Lucy, "I just think I have a knack for seeing other people's faults."

☆ ☆ ☆

Just before telling a juicy story about someone, a man said, "It's my policy never to say anything about anyone unless it's something good. And boy is this ever good!"

Dads

As they were pulling into the driveway after a month-long visit to her parents, a mother told her son, "Remember to run to Daddy first, and then to the dog."

☆ ☆ ☆

Three boys were heading home from school one day when one started the time-honored game of paternal one-upmanship. He said, "My dad's way faster than any of yours. He can throw a ninety-mile-an-hour fastball from the pitcher's mound and run and catch it just after it crosses the plate!"

One of the other boys said, "Oh yeah? Well, my dad can shoot an arrow from his bow and run to the target and hold it up to make sure the arrow hits the bull's-eye!"

The last boy said, "Your dads don't even come close to being as fast as mine. My dad works for the government, and even though he works every day until 4:00, he gets home at 3:30!"

A little girl wanted to know why her father brought home so much work. Her mother explained that he was unable to get it all done at the office.

The little girl then asked, "Then why don't they put him in a slower group?"

☆ ☆ ☆

On one of his rare visits home, a traveling salesman told his wife that he would take care of the kids if she wanted to go out with her friends.

When the time came, Dad put the kids to bed and settled down to read. One of the kids kept appearing at the bottom of the stairs, but Dad kept sending him back to bed.

An hour later, a neighbor lady came over looking for her son. The Dad was proceeding to inform her that his kids had been in bed for quite some time, when over the banister popped a little head, and a voice shouted, "I'm here, Mom, but he won't let me go home!"

☆ ☆ ☆

A little boy asked his father why his apple turned brown after he started to eat it.

His father said, "Because when the meat of the apple is exposed to air, the air causes it to oxidize, thus changing the molecular structure, which turns into a different color."

After a long silence, the boy asked, "Daddy, are you talking to me?"

Coming home from school, a boy asked his mother a question. She replied, "Why not wait until your dad comes home and ask him."

The little boy said, "But Mom, I don't want to know that much about it."

☆ ☆ ☆

"Mommy, if the stork brings babies and Santa Claus brings presents, and if the Lord give us our daily bread and Uncle Sam our Social Security, why do we keep Daddy around?"

☆ ☆ ☆

A young fellow away at college couldn't get home for Christmas. He sent his father a cheap present with a note, "Dear Dad, this isn't much, but it is all you could afford."

Dating

On their third date, the guy was astounded when the girl of his dreams accepted his hasty proposal of marriage.

"Gee, I. . .I'm so flattered," he stammered. "I know I certainly don't deserve you. I don't have much money, and I realize I'm not the greatest-looking fellow around, either."

"Oh, don't worry about all that," she said with a wave of her hand. "You'll be away at work twelve or fourteen hours every day."

✫ ✫ ✫

Sally explained why she married Tom instead of Bill.

"When I was with Bill, I thought he was one of the most charming, witty, and delightful people I'd ever met."

"Then why didn't you marry him?" she was asked.

"Because when I'm with Tom, he makes me feel like *I'm* the most charming, witty, and delightful person *he's* ever met."

106

A mother asked her daughter, "How come I don't see that boy around anymore?"

"Which one?" the daughter asked.

"You know, the one you couldn't live without!"

✫ ✫ ✫

"Your boyfriend stayed very late last night," the father admonished his daughter.

"Did the noise bother you, Dad?"

"No, but the long periods of silence did!"

✫ ✫ ✫

A father was speaking to the young man who'd been dating his daughter about his finances. "What will be your yearly income?" the father asked.

"Fifty thousand," the young man replied.

"Not too shabby. And when you add my daughter's forty thousand, that'll be a very comfortable income."

"Oh, I already counted her in the fifty!"

✫ ✫ ✫

The Tower of London said to the Tower of Pisa: "If you have the inclination, I have the time."

Definitions

acupuncturist: *a Chinese doctor who quietly does his jab.*

alarm clock: *a device to scare the daylights into you.*

antique: *an item your grandparents bought, your parents got rid of, and you're buying again.*

argument: *a fight over who can get in the last word first.*

bargain: *something that's so cheap you can't resist it, even though you can't use it and don't really want it.*

beta tester: *anyone who uses a computer program.*

business meeting: *a time for people to talk about what they're supposed to be doing.*

courtesy: *the art of yawning with your mouth closed.*

etc.: *an abbreviation used to make people think you have additional information.*

experience: *something you've acquired after it's too late to do you much good.*

expert: *someone who knows the answers—assuming you ask the right questions.*

expiration: *the process of not breathing.*

furlough: *snore duty.*

goblet: *a young turkey.*

gossipers: *people who believe anything they overhear.*

graduate school: *the approximate point at which a university student ceases dependency on parents and commences dependency on spouse.*

import: *an inland seaport.*

impossibility: *something no one can do until someone does it.*

know-it-all: *a person who knows everything there is to know about nothing.*

laughing stock: *cattle with a sense of humor.*

love: *what happens when imagination overpowers common sense.*

low mileage: *what you get when your car won't start.*

middle age: *when you're sitting home alone on Friday night and you hope the phone* doesn't *ring.*

miser: *a person who lives poor and dies rich.*

money: *a device by which parents stay in touch with their children at college.*

mundane: *the day after a wonderful weekend.*

nail: *what amateur carpenters replace with their thumb while the hammer is in motion.*

nothing: *the presence of absence.*

nuclear scientist: *a professional with a lot of ions in the fire.*

opportunist: *a mail carrier who enjoys the view when treed by a dog.*

opportunity: *something that knocks, but doesn't turn the door handle.*

optimist: *someone blithely ignorant of how serious a crisis really is.*

orthodontist: *a doctor who braces children and straps parents.*

oxygen: *a little-used form of the word "ox."*

pessimist: *a former optimist.*

phonetic: *an example of a word that isn't spelled the way it sounds.*

practical nurse: *a caregiver who marries a wealthy patient.*

quality control: *corporate term for "nagging."*

quicksilver: *what the Lone Ranger says when he needs to go fast.*

Rome: *what buffalo do.*

scorekeeper: *the symphony orchestra's librarian.*

shin: *a device for finding furniture in the dark.*

spice: *plural of spouse.*

steering committee: *a panel of individuals who aren't capable of driving by themselves.*

subordinate clause: *the grammatically correct term for Santa Claus's assistant.*

tact: *the knack for knowing exactly what not to say.*

teamwork: *getting a group of individuals to do what one person tells them to.*

time: *the component of life that keeps everything bad from happening to you all at once.*

tragic opera: *a musical–theatrical performance in which most of the characters sing, then die.*

unbreakable: *an adjective used to describe many toys—with the implied disclaimer that any warranties are voided where children are present.*

upward adjustment: *a price increase.*

vegetarian: *a person who refuses to eat meat in public.*

wake-up call: *the issue of mind over mattress.*

wastebasket: *a receptacle near which trash is tossed.*

wide receiver: *a twelve-foot satellite dish.*

yacht: *a floating credit liability.*

Diet and Exercise

Jeff: Why are you so eager to meet the right woman, settle down and get married?
Mike: So I can stop dieting.

☆　☆　☆

If I can lose thirty pounds, I'll be down to the weight I never thought I would be up to.

☆　☆　☆

"I'm starting a new diet the doctor prescribed."
　"What inspired that?"
　"I'm sick and tired of being thick and tired."

☆　☆　☆

My doctor told me that jogging would add years to my life. I think he was right. I feel ten years older already.

Cookbooks are the biggest sellers, and diet books are second. The moral of the story is "Don't eat what you just learned to cook."

☆　☆　☆

I spent a fortune on a trampoline.
A stationary bike and a rowing machine
Complete with gadgets to read my pulse,
And others to show the miles I've charted—
But they left off the gadget to get me started.

☆　☆　☆

"I thought you said you were counting calories," remarked Mrs. Bowker, scowling as her friend Mrs. Halburton enjoyed her second chocolate shake at the ice cream shop.

"I am indeed," said Mrs. Halburton between slurps. "So far today, this makes 7,750."

☆　☆　☆

A couple were enjoying a dinner party at the home of friends. Near the end of the meal, the wife slapped her husband's arm.

"That's the third time you've gone for dessert," she said. "The hostess must think you're an absolute pig."

"I doubt that," the husband said. "I've been telling her it's for you."

"Have you heard about the amazing new pasta diet?"

"No. What's involved?"

"It's so simple! You simply learn to walk pasta da refrigerator without stopping, and pasta da cookie jar, and pasta da cupboard. . ."

☆ ☆ ☆

I bend a sympathetic ear
To other people's moans
However dull it is to hear
Their real or fancied groans.
I pay to every gloomy line
Attention undiminished
Because I plan to start on mine
The moment theirs are finished.

☆ ☆ ☆

The Six Commandments of Satchel Paige
1. Avoid fried food, which angers the blood.
2. When your stomach disputes you, lie down and pacify it with cool thoughts.
3. Go light on the vices, like carryin' on at night in society, 'cause the social ramble ain't restful.
4. Avoid running at all times.
5. Keep your juices flowin' by janglin' gently as you move around.
6. Never look back; something might be gainin' on you.

One man was determined to shed some pounds. Soon, however, the agony of deprivation became so intense that he talked himself into thinking maybe God wanted him to have a little relief. He decided to test his theory. He told himself that if there was a parking place in front of the bakery, which was usually crowded with cars, it would mean that, yes, God wanted him to indulge.

Well, sure enough, on his tenth trip around the block, there was a parking place right in front of the door.

Dimwitties

A man ordered the plans for a tree house for his children. Instead, he received the plans for a sailboat. In reply to his angry letter of complaint, the company wrote, "We can understand your anger about this mistake, but it was nothing compared to the man who went out on the lake and tried to sail a tree house."

✩ ✩ ✩

Two friends rented a boat and went fishing in the lake. The first day, they caught thirty fish. As they were preparing to go in to shore, one man said to the other, "Let's mark this spot so we can come here again tomorrow."

The next day, when they were driving to rent the boat, the same one said, "Did you mark that spot?"

His friend replied, "Yeah, I put a big X on the bottom of the boat."

The first one said, "That was dumb. What if we don't get the same boat today?"

Joe was in court, charged with parking in a restricted area. The judge asked him if he had anything to say in his defense. "They should not put up such misleading notices," Joe said. "It read: FINE FOR PARKING HERE."

✫ ✫ ✫

"I don't think my right signal light is working," said Pam, stopping her car at a traffic light one evening. Asking brother Sam to check it, she flipped the blinker switch. Sam stuck his head out the passenger's window and reported, "It's working. . . . Wait a minute. . . . It's working. . . . Wait a minute. . . . It's working. . . ."

✫ ✫ ✫

A couple was gathering items for a garage sale before relocating to a new home.

"Bah, here's a totally worthless item," said the husband bringing a fire extinguisher out of the closet.

"Why do you say it's worthless?"

"Well, we bought it at least five years ago, and we've never used it at all."

✫ ✫ ✫

An East coast couple visited Los Angeles. "It sure is hot here," one of them commented. "You have to remember," the other replied, "we're 3,000 miles from the ocean."

Two ditch diggers were upset because they did all the hard work yet received only one-tenth of the pay of the crew boss. Finally, deciding to confront his boss, one guy climbed out of the ditch and went over to the foreman, who was leaning against a tree reading the sports page.

"How come we do all the hard work while you sit there reading the paper and earn ten times as much?" he demanded.

"Intelligence," the crew boss answered. "Let me give you an example." He put his hand in front of the tree. "See my hand?" Hit it as hard as you can."

The ditch digger took a mighty swing, but the boss moved his hand at the last second, and the man's fist slammed into the tree.

"See what I mean?" the foreman said.

The ditch digger returned to work and his friend eagerly questioned him about what the foreman had said.

"It's a matter of intelligence," the first guy said. "Let me give you an example. He held his hand up in front of his face. "Hit my hand as hard as you can."

☆ ☆ ☆

A man took a parcel notice to the post office counter and asked for his package. The clerk was gone for several minutes, searching the rear of the post office for the package. At last, the clerk returned, scrutinizing the label of a large, fat, battered manila envelope.

"I think this one may be yours," the clerk said, "but the name seems to be obliterated."

"It's not mine then," said the customer. "My name is Welles."

A guy was walking down the street and passed a hardware store that was advertising a sale on a chainsaw capable of cutting seven hundred trees in seven hours. The guy thought that was a great deal and decided to buy one.

The next day, he came back with the saw and complained to the salesman that the thing didn't come close to chopping down the seven hundred trees the ad said it would.

"Well," said the salesman, "let's test it out back."

Finding a log, the salesman pulled the starter cord and the saw roared to life.

"What's that noise?" asked the customer.

☆ ☆ ☆

Coming in from a drenching rain, a gentleman hung his coat on a crowded rack in the waiting room of a doctor's office. He called at the desk and was admitted shortly afterward for his scheduled appointment.

An hour and a half later, he emerged from his checkup and went to the rack for his coat. Plundering through the collection of wraps, he became annoyed, then angry. He was slinging coats on the floor furiously when the receptionist came to his assistance.

"I believe this one's yours, Mr. Tettleby," she said politely, holding up his coat. "See? It has your initials on the liner."

"Certainly not," refuted Mr. Tettleby. "My coat was soaking wet."

In the Midwest, storm cellars are common precautions for the tornados that occasionally come. One man spent a good deal of money for one, and every time there was a warning, he got in it, but there was never any damage to his property. He began to wonder if he had spent his money for nothing. One day, however, he came forth to find his barn ripped apart by the wind. "Now that," he said, looking up at the sky, "is more like it."

Doctors and Dentists

A particular patient called on his doctor frequently, usually with imaginary ailments.

"Doc, you gotta help me," he said. "I'm really worried this time. This is serious."

"Okay, Phil. What seems to be the problem?"

"I think I'm becoming a hypochondriac."

☆ ☆ ☆

Doctor: "What seems to be the problem with little Micah today?"

Panicked Parent: "We think he swallowed a bullet!"

Doctor: "For heaven's sake, stop pointing him at me!"

☆ ☆ ☆

Doctor: "How are you feeling?"

Patient: "I feel a whole lot more like I do now than I did a little while ago."

Doctor: "That's a horrible gash on your skull. What happened?"

Child: "My sister hit me with some tomatoes."

Doctor: "That's incredible. I've never seen a tomato cut before."

Child: "Well, these were in a can."

☆ ☆ ☆

The doctor was amazed at the health and durability of Mrs. Sedgefield, age ninety-two. "What's your secret to long life and health?" he asked her.

"Honey and arithmetic."

"What do you mean, honey and arithmetic?"

"Every morning since I was a baby, I've had a spoonful of honey. If you take that every day, and then multiply it by 33,580 days, you'll live to be ninety-two, just like me."

☆ ☆ ☆

Doctor: "So you haven't been able to sleep well?"

Patient: "I sleep fine during the night, but during my afternoon naps, I just can't keep my eyes closed."

☆ ☆ ☆

"Doc, it's my husband!" shrieked a woman into the phone. "I served lasagna for dinner last night, and this morning he's turned all blue!"

"Sing him a song," suggested the doctor. "Tell him a joke. That'll cheer him up."

A young man brought his wife to a small town doctor's office in an emergency. The nurses escorted the woman to the examination area, and the husband anxiously took a seat in the lobby.

For the next few minutes, he could hear the doctor bark an unsettling string of orders to the staff. First it was "Knife!" Then "Screwdriver!" Then "Pliers!"

When he heard "Sledgehammer!" the young man could bear the tension no longer. He burst into the examination room and shrieked, "Doctor, what's *wrong* with her?"

"We have no idea," the doctor said. "Right now, we're still trying to open the medicine cabinet."

☆　☆　☆

My dentist said to me the other day, "I have some good news and some bad news."

I said, "What's the bad news?"

"You need root-canal work."

"What's the good news?"

"I birdied two holes yesterday!"

☆　☆　☆

Emergency Room Receptionist: "What's the problem?"

Incoming Patient: "These pains in my sides and back. I feel like I have double pneumonia."

Receptionist: "We have only single beds. Which side would you like treated?"

"I've had horrible indigestion for the past two days," a patient said.

"And what have you been doing for it?" asked the doctor.

"Taking an antacid twice a day and drinking nothing but milk," said the patient.

"Good—exactly what I would have suggested myself. That'll be $50."

☆ ☆ ☆

Did you have a good time at the dentist?

It was a scream!

☆ ☆ ☆

My dentist saves me a lot of money. When my X-rays show a lot of cavities, he touches them up.

☆ ☆ ☆

A pharmacist was squinting and holding the prescription slip up to the light. Finally, she took up a magnifier in a futile effort to read it.

"We don't think too highly of this particular doctor," she told the customer, "but there's one thing he obviously can do better than anyone else on the planet."

"What's that?"

"Read his own handwriting."

An auto mechanic in the hospital was chatting nervously with his surgeon while being prepped for an operation. "Sometimes I wish I'd gone into your line of work," he told the doctor. "Everything you doctors do is so cut and dried and tidy. With me, I spend half a day taking an engine apart and putting it back together, and it seems I always have a couple of parts left over."

"Yes," said the surgeon. "I know the feeling."

☆　☆　☆

Doctor: "What seems to be the problem?"
Patient: "It's my husband. He's swallowed my fountain pen."
Doctor: "That's serious. Have you done anything about it?"
Patient: "Yes. I've made him buy me a new one."

☆　☆　☆

Doctors in the emergency room examined the incoming patient, a hit-and-run victim, with concern. Several broken ribs, a fractured femur, and various other internal and external injuries indicated tedious surgical procedures were in order. It was amazing the patient was momentarily conscious.

"Are you allergic to anything," one doctor asked.

"Yes," she replied weakly.

"What's that?"

"Oncoming trucks."

Patient: "Doc, what do you recommend for an insomniac like me?"

Doctor: "A good night's sleep."

A doctor's receptionist answered the phone and was screamed at by an excited man at the other end of the line.

"My wife's in labor!" he yelled. "I think she's going to deliver any minute now."

"Please calm down," the receptionist said. "Try to relax and give me some basic information. Is this her first child?"

"No, no! I'm her husband!"

Dogs

A salesman approached the gate of a farmyard and was about to enter when he noticed a large dog under a shade bush, eyeing him. The salesman called out to see if anyone was home.

The farmer and his wife came to the front door. "Come on in," said the farmer with a friendly gesture.

"What about the dog?" asked the salesman, hesitating. "Will he bite?"

"Don't know. We just got 'im yesterday, and we're right eager to find out."

☆ ☆ ☆

A couple at a sprawling, three-state dog show was about to leave when they realized they hadn't yet seen any Labrador Retrievers. The man asked an attendant, "Can you tell us where to find the Labs?"

The attendant scratched his head. "Oh," he said blankly. "Next building. Men's on the right, ladies' on the left."

A man was playing chess with his dog on the backyard picnic table. A neighbor noticed. "Wow, I've never seen a dog play chess before. She must be very smart."

"Hah!" scoffed the dog's owner. "She's not so smart. I've beaten her four out of five games."

☆ ☆ ☆

A mother, much against her better judgment, finally gave in and bought the children a dog with the understanding that they would take care of it. They named the dog Danny. It wasn't long before the mother was taking care of the dog all by herself. Since the children did not live up to their promise, she decided to sell Danny.

One of them said, "We'll miss him."

Another said, "If he wouldn't eat so much and wouldn't be so messy, could we keep him?"

Mom held her ground. "It's time to take Danny to his new home."

With one voice and in tearful outrage, the children reacted, "Danny? We thought you said Daddy."

☆ ☆ ☆

Walking home from school, a group of children watched a fire truck driving by. The company dog was sitting on the front seat. They began to discuss the dog's duties.

"They use him to keep back the crowds," one suggested.

"No, it's just for good luck," another said.

The discussion ended when one explained, "They use him to find the fire hydrant."

A little boy bought a box of detergent, telling the clerk he wanted it to wash his dog. The clerk told him to be very careful because it was very strong.

The next time the boy came in, the clerk asked him about his dog, and the boy said, "He died."

"Well, I told you that it was really too strong to wash a little dog," the clerk said.

"I don't think it was that," the boy explained. "I think it was the rinse cycle that got him."

☆ ☆ ☆

Two days after they'd moved into the neighborhood, the new family received a visit from a neighbor around the corner. "I'm very concerned," the neighbor said solemnly. "Your dogs are up barking all night long."

"Oh, they'll be quite all right," said the woman of the house. "They get plenty of sleep during the day."

☆ ☆ ☆

Mother caught little Davey feeding the dog under the table at suppertime again. "Davey," she fussed, "you know very well you're not supposed to feed the dog from our table food!"

"Yes, ma'am," Davey confessed, hanging his head.

"Don't you understand why we have that rule in our house?"

Davey thought a moment. "I guess it's because if the dog doesn't like the food, the stuff will end up on the floor and eventually rot."

A guy with a Doberman pinscher and a guy with a Chihuahua went for a walk one afternoon. After a while, they became hungry, and the guy with the Doberman says to the guy with the Chihuahua, "Let's go over to that restaurant and get something to eat."

The guy with the Chihuahua says, "We can't go in there. We've got our dogs with us."

The guy with the Doberman says, "Just follow my lead."

They walk over to the restaurant. As they reach the front door, the guy with the Doberman pinscher puts on a pair of dark glasses and walks in.

The maitre d' says, "Excuse me, sir, but no pets allowed."

The guy with the Doberman says, "You don't understand. This is my seeing-eye dog."

The maitre d' says, "A Doberman pinscher?"

The man replies, "Yes, they're using them now, and they're excellent guide dogs."

The maitre d' shrugs and says, "Okay, come on in."

The guy with the Chihuahua sees all this and figures, "Why not?" So he puts on a pair of dark glasses and walks into the restaurant.

The maitre d' says, "Excuse me, sir, but no pets allowed."

The guy with the Chihuahua replies, "You don't understand. This is my seeing-eye dog."

The maitre d' says, "A Chihuahua?"

The man with the dog says, "They gave me a Chihuahua?"

A notice in a weekly newspaper advertised bulldog puppies. "Cute, already housebroken," the advertiser promised. "Eat most any food you put in front of them. Love children."

☆ ☆ ☆

The phone rang at two o'clock in the morning. Groggily, the man of the house lifted the receiver and heard, "This is 330 Woodvine, next block over. Your dog's been howling for the last thirty minutes, and we can't get to sleep. Shut that animal up!"

Without waiting for a response, the caller hung up the phone.

The next night at 2 A.M., the aroused neighbor dialed up 330 Woodvine. When the owner answered, he pleasantly informed him, "We don't own a dog," and hung up.

Drivers

A driving student was poring through the handbook just before taking the written exam. Suddenly, he got up and hurried from the training room.

"Hey, where are you going?" the instructor demanded.

"I'm outta here, man. Gotta phone my parents, like, right now!"

"What's the matter? Don't you want to earn your driver's license?"

"Doesn't matter. First thing we have to do is move, and I mean *today*!"

"Move? You mean move your family?"

"Yep. Lock, stock and motorcycle. Find a new house."

"What on earth for?"

"It says in that book that 90 percent of all traffic fatalities in the United States occur within five miles of home."

"My Dad must be a pretty bad driver," said Brad.

"What do you mean?" asked Bret.

"I was with him when he got pulled over for speeding yesterday. The officer recognized him and wrote him a season ticket."

☆ ☆ ☆

An elderly lady driving a big, new, expensive car was preparing to back into a parallel parking space when suddenly, a young man in a small sports car zoomed into the space.

The lady charged out of her car and angrily demanded to know why he had done that when it was obvious she was trying to park there.

His response was simply, "Because I'm young and I'm quick."

When he came back a few minutes later, the lady was using her luxury car as a battering ram against the little sports car. Now the young man was angry and asked her why she was wrecking his car.

Her response was simply, "Because I'm old and I'm rich."

☆ ☆ ☆

A woman was applying for the renewal of her driver's license. She was asked by the inspector, "Have you ever been judged insane or feebleminded?" He paused and smiled before adding, "That is, by anyone other than your own children?"

A patrol officer chased down a speeder after a thirty-mile adventure on the interstate—but only after the speeder ran out of gas.

"Congratulations," said the officer sarcastically. "You hit 163 miles per hour. I didn't think a little subcompact like that could give me such a run."

"And congratulations to you. I didn't think you could keep up."

☆ ☆ ☆

A driver stopped beside a pedestrian in a tiny, remote town. Lost and in a hurry, the driver had no desire to engage in conversation with the locals; he only wanted quick directions.

"Hey, old timer," he snapped. "Can you tell me how to get to Portland?"

"Yep," the man replied, before crossing the street and disappearing inside a shop door.

☆ ☆ ☆

Some teenage friends were marveling at the scene of an accident from which one of them had miraculously walked away without a scratch the night before.

"Wow, that was some smash-up," said one.

"Totaled the car," said another.

"How'd it happen?" asked a third.

The victim pointed to a tilted telephone pole. "See that?"

"Yeah."

"I didn't."

A highway patrolman stopped a car for flagrantly speeding on I-95.

"Don't you know the speed limit?" he asked.

"Sure. It's ninety-five. It's posted every few miles."

"That's the highway number, not the speed limit."

"I realized it was kinda fast—but I figured it was the government's way of letting people make up for lost time."

"Lost time? What do you mean?"

"Well, if those aren't speed limit signs, then I guess I spent the first half of the day on Interstate Twenty."

☆　☆　☆

"I clocked you doing ninety-six miles an hour, buddy. Something wrong?"

"Yes, officer. I forgot to plug in my radar detector."

☆　☆　☆

A team of paramedics loaded a dazed auto accident victim into the ambulance.

"I don't understand it," the stunned patient moaned. "I'm sure I had the right-of-way."

"Yes," replied a medic, "but the other driver had the eighteen-wheeler."

☆　☆　☆

"I'm only giving you a warning," said the policeman, handing a form to a beautiful young woman he'd stopped for speeding.

"Oh, thank you so much, officer!" she said, folding the warning ticket neatly into her purse. "I collect these."

Economics

A young couple were about to buy an electric grill and put it on their credit card. They debated whether to select the economy model or the deluxe unit that had every imaginable convenience.

"Ah, let's go ahead and get the big one," said the husband.

"Yeah," said his wife. "It won't really cost us any more. We'll just have to pay a little longer."

✧ ✧ ✧

Many investors require a stockbroker one day and a pawnbroker the next.

✧ ✧ ✧

Have you heard about the hot new credit plan? You put 100 percent down and have no monthly payments!

Did you ever wonder why hamburger buns come eight to a package—when hamburger patties come in packages of five or ten?

☆ ☆ ☆

A woman was extremely impressed with a gold watch in a jewelry shop. "You say this is only $29.95," she remarked to the jeweler. "There must be something wrong with it."

"No, madam. It's simply marked down to a dollar above cost."

"You're telling me you paid only $29 for it yourself?"

"That's correct, madam."

"Nonsense. If that's true, how could you possibly make a living?"

"You forget, madam, this is also a repair shop."

☆ ☆ ☆

Money talks, but it has a one-word vocabulary: *Good–bye*.

☆ ☆ ☆

After successfully getting their big line items approved in the congressional spending package, two lobbyists were celebrating at a Washington restaurant.

"You know," mused one, "it's a crying shame our grandchildren and great-grandchildren haven't been born yet so they can see the terrific things the government's doing with their money."

English Signs

Sign in a laundromat: "Automatic Washing Machines: Please remove all your clothes when the light goes out."

☆ ☆ ☆

Sign in a Soho office: "Would the person who removed the stepladder yesterday kindly bring it back—or further steps will be taken."

☆ ☆ ☆

Sign in an office kitchen: "After the tea break, staff should empty the teapot and stand upside down on the drain-board."

☆ ☆ ☆

Sign outside a disco: "Smarts. The Most Exclusive Disco in Town. Everyone Welcome."

Notice in health food shop window: "Closed Due to Illness."

✩ ✩ ✩

Sign outside a new town hall, which was to be officially opened by the Prince of Wales: "The Town Hall Is Closed Until The Opening. It Will Remain Closed After The Opening, And Will Open Tomorrow."

✩ ✩ ✩

Sign in a London department store: "Bargain Basement Upstairs."

✩ ✩ ✩

Warning sign: "Quicksand. Any Person Passing This Point Will Be Drowned. By Order of the District Council."

✩ ✩ ✩

Notice sent to residents of a Wiltshire parish: "Due to increasing problems with litter, louts, and vandals, we must ask anyone with relatives buried in the graveyard to do their best to keep them in order."

✩ ✩ ✩

Notice in a field: "The Farmer Allows Walkers To Cross The Field, But The Bull Charges."

Sign on a motorway garage: "Please Do Not Smoke Near Our Petrol Pumps. Your Life May Not Be Worth Much, But Our Petrol Is."

✫ ✫ ✫

Sign outside a secondhand shop: "We Exchange Anything: Bicycles, Washing Machines, etc. Bring your wife along and get a wonderful bargain."

✫ ✫ ✫

Sign on a repair shop door: "We Can Fix Anything. (Please Knock Hard on the Door—The Bell Doesn't Work.)"

✫ ✫ ✫

Sign at Norfolk farm gate: "Beware! I Shoot Every Tenth Trespasser and the Ninth One Just Left."

Family Ties

A farmer's wife went into a coma at home, and he summoned the doctor.

"She's gone," said the doc after examining the woman. "I'm very sorry. I'll call the funeral home for you."

The morticians carried the body down the porch steps and started to round the corner of the house into the driveway when the lead bearer suddenly lurched to avoid a holly bush, lost his balance and dropped his end of the stretcher. The jolt brought the woman back to consciousness. In a week, she'd made a full recovery and was back at the farm.

Several years later, she again went into a coma. This time, the doctor sadly assured her husband she was unquestionably dead.

The undertakers were summoned. As the stretcher bearers inched down the steps and headed for the driveway with the corpse, the farmer cautioned, "Watch out for that holly bush."

Mother was amused when she heard her six-year-old son whining to a friend: "I don't get it. My sister insists she has three brothers. But I'm in the same family, and I count only two brothers. . . ."

☆ ☆ ☆

She: "Our problem is that we're just not
    communicating."
He: "I don't wanna discuss it."

☆ ☆ ☆

A very successful businessman had a meeting with his new son-in-law. "I love my daughter," he said, "and now I welcome you into the family. To show how much we care for you, I'm making you a fifty-fifty partner in my business. All you have to do is go to the factory every day and learn the operations."

The son-in-law interrupted him. "I hate factories. I can't stand all the noise."

"I see," replied the father-in-law. "Well then, you'll work in the office and take care of some of those operations."

"I hate office work," countered the young man. "I can't stand being stuck behind a desk all day."

"Wait a minute," the exasperated father-in-law said, "I just made you half owner of a multimillion dollar money making organization, but you say you don't like factories and won't work in the office. What am I going to do with you?"

"Easy," said the smug son-in-law. "Buy me out."

When he went to visit his cousin in the big city, Farmer Dan was amazed at the dozens of cats loitering around the apartment complex. "Why don't you shoo 'em?" he asked his cousin.

"Here in town, we let the cats go barefoot."

✰ ✰ ✰

A woman was deeply depressed after her husband's death—until the insurance agent appeared in a few weeks with a $300,000 benefit check.

"I do believe," she confided to a friend, "I'd give $5,000 to have him back."

✰ ✰ ✰

The new bride had spent two hours preparing her first breakfast. She sat at the table, eagerly watching as her husband slowly savored each forkful.

"How was it, honey?" she asked when he'd finished.

"Well," he began thoughtfully, wiping his lips, "you probably could have beaten the eggshells a little longer. But on the whole, it was a good start."

✰ ✰ ✰

A young couple were discussing what to name their newborn son.

"I really like the name Ryan," the mother said.

"Nah," said her husband. "Every Tom, Dick, and Harry these days is called Ryan."

"Now, Charles, come give your old aunt a kiss before she goes," Aunt Meg said, putting on her gloves.

Charles shook his head.

"Come, now, Charles." She took a quarter from her purse and smiled. "I'll give you this if you'll just give me one little kiss on the cheek, like a good boy."

"Nah," Charles said. "Mom gives me that much just for eating Brussels sprouts."

☆ ☆ ☆

Smith: "I understand the Family Court social worker was at your house asking questions the other day."

Jones: "Yeah, my son was telling everyone at school he came from a broken home."

Smith: "Broken home? I thought you and Angie were happily married."

Jones: "We are. But the cement's coming loose between the blocks in our basement."

☆ ☆ ☆

A man was lounging in the living room, reading a magazine, when his wife crowded in the front door with bulging bags from a trip to the mall.

"I thought you were only going window shopping," he teased.

"That's right. I have the new curtains for the kitchen—and a matching bread box, can opener, cutlery set, spice rack. . . ."

Mrs. Wade was trying to be tactful with her friend Mrs. Griffin. "Now that your son George has turned thirty, don't you think it's time he decided what to do with his life?"

"Oh, he's at a very difficult age," Mrs. Griffin said.

"What do you mean?"

"Why, he's simply caught in limbo: too old to live at home with us, but too young to draw Social Security."

☆ ☆ ☆

Grandson: "Grandma, how many brothers and sisters did you have?"

Grandma: "Eleven brothers and eight sisters."

Grandson: "Wow! I bet yours was the biggest family in the whole town."

Grandma: "Yes. I expect that's why they built the new school next to our house."

☆ ☆ ☆

At three o'clock in the morning, a young wife shook her husband awake.

"What is it?" he asked groggily.

"The baby," she reminded him.

The husband sat up and listened for a full minute. "But I don't hear her crying," he protested.

"I know. It's your turn to go see why not."

Two cousins were having a friendly chat when one blurted, out of the blue, "Man, I need to borrow $100 from somebody by the end of the week."

"Really?"

"I sure do. Don't know who to turn to, either."

"Whew! It sounded for a moment like you were gonna turn to me."

☆ ☆ ☆

A beloved matron of the town was dying. Her family stood by, reflecting on her many wonderful qualities.

"She was the perfect mother," said one grown daughter. "Always there, always caring, always loving—but not to be disobeyed."

"She was the same to the whole community," said a son. "Everyone in town, I believe, regarded her as if she were their own mother."

"She sure knew how to cook!" chirped a grandson, sending a ripple of subdued chuckles through the morose gathering.

"And she was always the first to volunteer," added her minister.

The old woman turned her head on the pillow to face them. She moaned, "Motherhood. Cooking. Volunteering. Not one comment about how wonderfully modest I am."

Al: "You sure seem unhappy."

Val: "Yep. Living with my mother-in-law is really stressful. She's constantly fussing at both me and my wife."

Al: "Well, if worse comes to worst, you may have to ask her to move out."

Val: "I don't think we can do that. It's her house."

Farmers

Two farmers were commiserating about the long drought.

"It's so dry now, my pond water's about gone."

"Mine, too. And I hear over in Branchville, the Baptist church has gone to sprinkling and the Methodists are wringing cactus juice onto a handkerchief."

✫ ✫ ✫

A farm is a place where you can get rich overnight, assuming you strike oil.

✫ ✫ ✫

A farmer chided his teenage grandson, "Your generation has gotten lazy. When I was fifteen, I thought nothing of getting up at daybreak to milk the cows."

"I don't think much of it, either," replied the youth.

Farmer Joe was in a traffic accident with a semi-truck. After putting up with nagging injuries for several weeks, he decided to take the trucking company to court.

During the trial, the trucking company's high-powered lawyer questioned farmer Joe harshly. "Didn't you say, at the scene of the accident, 'I'm fine'?" questioned the attorney.

Farmer Joe responded, "Well, I'll tell you what happened. I had just loaded my favorite mule Bessie into the. . ."

"I didn't ask for a story," the lawyer snapped. "Just answer my question. Did you not say, at the scene of the accident, 'I'm fine'?"

Farmer Joe replied, "Well, I had just got Bessie into the trailer and I was driving down the road. . ."

The lawyer interrupted again and said, "Judge, I am trying to establish the fact that, at the scene of the accident, this man told the highway patrolman on the scene that he was just fine. Now, several weeks after the accident, he is trying to sue my client. I believe he is a fraud. Please tell him to simply answer the question."

By this time the judge was fairly interested in Farmer Joe's answer, and said to the lawyer, "I'd like to hear what he has to say about his favorite mule Bessie."

Joe thanked the judge and proceeded, "Well, as I was saying, I had just loaded Bessie, my favorite mule, into the trailer and was driving her down the highway when this huge semi-truck and trailer ran the stop sign and smacked my truck right in the side. I was thrown into one ditch and Bessie was thrown into the other. I was hurting real bad and didn't want to move. However, I could hear old Bessie moaning and groaning. I knew she was in terrible shape just by her whining. Shortly after the accident a highway patrolman came on the scene. He could hear Bessie moaning and groaning so he went over to her, and after looking at her, he took out his gun and shot her between the eyes. Then the patrolman came across the road with his gun in his hand and looked at me. He said, "Your mule was in such bad shape I had to shoot her. How are you feeling?"

☆ ☆ ☆

A city fellow came to a fork in a country road. "Hey, old-timer," he shouted to a farmer who was working out in his field. "I'm heading to Brownsville. Does it make any difference which road I take?"

The old man answered, "Not to me, it don't."

☆ ☆ ☆

Farmer Brown: "Did you lose much in that last tornado?"
Farmer Jones: "Lost the henhouse and all the chickens. But that was all right—I ended up with three new cows and somebody's pickup truck."

A school class was on a field trip to the farm.

"Look, look!" cried a student, pointing. "There's a little cow with no horns! All the other cows have horns. Why doesn't this one?"

The farmer drawled an explanation. "There are a lot of reasons some cows don't have horns," he said. "It might depend on the breed; some cattle breeds are horned and some aren't. Or it could be the cow's age; some don't grow horns until they're adults. And in some cases, cows that once had horns have lost them in collisions, or their owners have removed them for one reason or another.

"But in the case of this young cow here, it doesn't have horns because it's a colt."

☆　☆　☆

Farmer Tanner rang up a neighbor on the telephone. "My best milking cow has a fever," he said. "How did you treat your ol' Bessie when she got sick last winter?"

"Well, I made up a mixture of half cod liver oil and half turpentine, and put it in with her food once a day for four days."

"Thanks. I'll try it."

Farmer Tanner hung up the phone and proceeded to treat his cow. Shockingly, after four days of the medicine compound, the cow died.

He rang up his neighbor again. "Hey, I did exactly what you said with the cod liver oil and turpentine mixture, but my cow just died."

"Yep. So did ol' Bessie."

"I want to start a garden, but my yard's a little problematic," a customer told the proprietor at the yard and garden center. "I get blazing afternoon sunshine for about two hours, but otherwise it's all shade."

"What kind of soil?" asked the proprietor.

"Hard clay, lot of rocks. What do you recommend I plant?"

"Hmmm," mused the store owner. "Why don't you look down Aisle B? We've got a big new supply of birdbaths and flagpoles. . . ."

☆ ☆ ☆

A life insurance salesman was standing beside a tractor trying to sell a farmer a policy, but the farmer told him, "No, sir, I want no life insurance. When I die, I want it to be a sad day for everybody."

☆ ☆ ☆

Two farmers were in a bragging match about their produce.

"The eggs I get from my hens," said one, "are so big it takes just one to make a cake."

"Well, the ones I get are so big it takes just ten to make a dozen."

☆ ☆ ☆

"You know," said the farmer to his wife, "with all the additives they're putting in our milk these days, don't you reckon it makes old Bessie feel right deficient?"

A stranger frantically ran up to a farmer's door, pounded his fist and demanded, "Where's the nearest railroad station, and what time's the next train to the city?"

The farmer thought a moment. "Cut through my back hayfield, and you ought to reach the crossroads station in time for the 5:40. Actually, if my bull spots you, I expect you'll make the 5:15."

☆ ☆ ☆

A visitor to a farm was astounded to see brown bundles of feathers zooming around the barnyard, so fast they couldn't be seen clearly. "What in the world are those things?" he asked, somewhat alarmed.

"Those are my four-legged chickens," the farmer said. "I've been breedin' 'em. Quick, ain't they?"

"Yes, but why do you want four-legged chickens?"

"Cuz me and my wife and our two boys all like the drumstick. When we have fried chicken, there'll be a leg for each of us."

"Does it taste like normal fried chicken?"

"Don't know yet. We haven't been able to catch one."

☆ ☆ ☆

A farmer on his deathbed asked, "Are you there, dear wife?"

She answered, "Of course I am, my love."

Then he asked, "Are you there, beloved son?"

"Yes, of course I'm here, Father."

The man opened his eyes, gathered all his strength, and yelled, "Then who the dickens is milking the cows?"

First Aid

"I tried to give him artificial respiration," a boy who had pulled his little brother out of the lake was telling his mother, "but he kept getting up and walking away."

☆　☆　☆

"I was going for a walk this morning," a lady told her husband, "when I saw this poor man lying on the sidewalk in pretty bad condition. Fortunately, all my first-aid training came back to me and I bent down and put my head between my knees to keep from fainting."

Fishing

It was a fine way to spend the day—wading a favorite trout stream after placing several hooks into deep, dark pools. The only problem was he was playing golf.

☆ ☆ ☆

"I promised my wife I'd turn over a new leaf," Earl said. "From now on, I'm gonna fish in moderation."

☆ ☆ ☆

A man and his wife were in a boat on a lake. While the man fished, his wife read a book, shading herself with an umbrella.

The game warden motored up. "Don't you know this is a private lake?" the warden told the man. "It would be breaking the law to take any fish from here."

"Actually, officer," the wife intervened, "for him, it would be miraculous."

What happens to lying fishermen when they die?
They lie still.

☆ ☆ ☆

The determined angler staggered up to the counter with an armload of the latest gear. As the cashier was ringing up the total, which came to several hundred dollars, the angler commented, "You know, you could save me an awful lot of money if you'd just start selling fish here."

☆ ☆ ☆

The preacher, who was an ardent fisherman, performed a wedding. He asked the groom, "Do you promise to love, honor, and cherish this woman?"

He answered, "I do."

Then turning to the bride, he said, "Okay, reel him in."

☆ ☆ ☆

"What is your favorite parable?" the Sunday school teacher asked.

A boy answered, "I like the one where everybody loafs and fishes."

☆ ☆ ☆

The minister confronted Jim. "I hear you went to the ball game."

"That's a lie," Jim told him, "and here's a string of fish to prove it."

Angler's motto: "I only fish on days that end in *y*."

☆ ☆ ☆

A sporting goods store had just put up a large display of expensive fishing tackle. A customer picked up one of the newest lures and inspected the gleaming metal and plastic. "Do the fish really go for these things?" he asked the salesman.

"Dunno," the clerk replied. "We don't sell 'em to the fish."

Forgetfulness

The late Supreme Court Justice Oliver Wendell Holmes once found himself on a train, but couldn't locate his ticket. While the conductor watched, smiling, the eighty-eight-year-old justice searched through all his pockets without success.

Of course, the conductor recognized the distinguished jurist. So he said, "Mr. Holmes, don't worry. You don't need your ticket. You will probably find it when you get off the train, and I'm sure the Pennsylvania Railroad will trust you to mail it back later."

Justice Holmes looked up at the conductor with some irritation and said, "My dear man, that is not the problem at all. The problem is not where my ticket is. The problem is, where do I get off?"

✩ ✩ ✩

"Do you believe in the hereafter?" the minister asked a lady.

"I certainly do," she replied, "I often go in a room and say 'What am I here after?'"

159

Two men, who had been playing golf together for many years, were discussing the embarrassing problem of forgetting names. One of them said, "For example, what is your name? I can't think of it just now."

The other thought for a while and finally asked, "How soon do you need to know?"

☆ ☆ ☆

A man started up the stairs, stopped about halfway up, and couldn't remember what he was going upstairs for. "I'm going to sit right here on the step," he said to himself, "until I can remember what I'm going upstairs for."

After some thought, he couldn't remember if he was going up or down.

☆ ☆ ☆

An elderly couple was watching TV and the husband said, "I think a dish of ice cream would be nice."

The wife said, "Yes, dear, I'll get it."

He said, "You'd better write it down, or you'll forget."

"Nonsense."

"Oh yes, and let's have some chocolate sauce," the husband added.

"Yes, dear, I'll get it."

"OK," the husband said, "but you'd better write it down." Later, the wife returned, carrying bacon and eggs. The husband said, "I told you to write it down."

She asked, "Why? What did I forget?"

He replied, "You forgot the toast."

Frugality

One day, Jack Benny, George Burns, and Edgar Bergen were having lunch together. When the waiter brought the check, Benny said, "I'll take that." His friends were shocked, because Benny had a reputation for being tight. When it came to picking up a check, he had what might be called "a reach impediment." But on this occasion, he actually asked for the check.

On the way out of the restaurant, George Burns said, "It was certainly nice of you, Jack, to ask for the check."

Benny replied, "I did not ask for the check, and this is the last time I'll ever have lunch with a ventriloquist."

✩ ✩ ✩

"Your money or your life," the holdup man said to Jack Benny. Benny, who made a running gag out of being tight, didn't respond. "Come on," the thug said angrily, "Which is it, your money or your life?"

Benny answered, "I'm thinking it over."

Before leaving for Europe, a man drove his Rolls Royce to a downtown bank in New York. He went in and asked for a loan of five thousand dollars, offering his car as collateral. The loan officer gave him the money and promptly had the car driven into the bank's underground parking for safekeeping.

Two weeks later, the man returned. The interest on the loan came to $15.40, which he paid and then got the keys for his car.

Before he left, the loan officer said, "Why would a wealthy man like you need a five-thousand-dollar loan?"

The man smiled and said, "I don't need the money, but where else could I park my Rolls Royce in Manhattan for two weeks and pay only $15.40?"

☆　☆　☆

A woman was married to a parsimonious man. She had to fight for everything she got. One day she told him she was going window shopping and he said, "Look, but don't buy."

A few hours later, she came home with a dress. "What is this?" he fumed, "I thought I told you to look but not buy."

"Well," she explained, "I saw this lovely dress and thought I'd try it on. And when I did, the Devil said, 'It sure looks good on you.'"

"Right then you should have told him, 'Get thee behind me, Satan,'" her husband told her.

"I did," she answered, "but then he said, 'It looks good from the back, too.'"

Gifts

A little girl was asked what she was going to give her brother for Christmas.

"I don't know," she replied.

"What did you give him last year?"

She answered, "The chicken pox."

☆　☆　☆

A man spent several hours enduring long lines, surly clerks, and insane regulations at the Department of Motor Vehicles. On his way home, he stopped to pick up a gift for his son. He selected a baseball bat.

"Cash or charge?" the clerk asked.

"Cash," the man snapped. Then, apologizing for his rudeness, he explained, "I've just spent the entire afternoon at the motor vehicle bureau."

"I understand," the clerk replied and then asked, "Shall I gift wrap the bat? Or are you going back to the DMV?"

A wealthy man paid twenty-five thousand dollars for an exotic bird for his mother.

"How did you like the bird?" he asked her later.

She responded, "It was delicious."

☆　☆　☆

A man bought a fifty-dollar vase for two dollars because the handles had been broken off. He asked the salesperson to wrap it and send it to a friend, with the idea that the friend would think he had paid fifty dollars and that it was broken in mailing.

The friend wrote back, "Thank you for the lovely vase. It was so nice of you to wrap each piece separately."

God

A group of scientists got together and decided that humans had come a long way and no longer needed God. They picked one scientist to go tell God.

He said, "God, we've decided that we no longer need you. We can now clone people, we can walk on the moon—we can do everything."

God listened patiently, and after the scientist made his point, said, "I understand what you're saying, but before you dismiss me from your life, let's test your theory."

"Okay, great," the man replied. "What is the experiment?"

"We're going to create a man from the dust of the earth, just like I did back in the old days with Adam."

The scientist said, "Sure, no problem," and bent down to grab himself a handful of dirt.

"No, no, no," said the Lord. "You go get your own dirt."

I was at the beach with my children when my four-year-old son ran up to me, grabbed my hand, and led me to the shore where a seagull lay dead in the sand.

"Mommy, what happened to him?"

"He died and went to heaven," I replied.

My son thought a moment and then said, "And God threw him back down?"

☆ ☆ ☆

An airline attendant was asked by a friend if she believed in God. She said, "Let me tell you something that happened on one of my flights. I was serving the first-class cabin. Two men were sitting across the aisle from each other. One of them pulled a little cigarette-sized cigar out of his pocket and proceeded to light it. The man across the aisle said to him, 'Hey, you can't smoke on an airline.' The other man waved him aside and continued smoking his little cigar.

"A moment later I was walking down the aisle carrying a tray of drinks. A man pointed across the aisle and said, 'That man is smoking.' I looked. He was, and I told him, 'You can't smoke on an airliner.' He continued to smoke. I wondered what to do. Just then, the plane ran into turbulence and I pitched forward dumping the tray of drinks across him, extinguishing his cigar and getting him all wet. Then I fell backward into the lap of one of the most gorgeous men I've ever been near.

"Do you see why I believe in God?"

"You'll have to be quiet," a father told his little son. "We are in God's house now."

The little boy looked all around the church and asked his father, "Which door will God be coming in?"

☆ ☆ ☆

A young man was talking to God. "How long is a million years to You?" he asked.

"A million years to me is like a single second to you," God replied.

"How much is a million dollars to You?" the young man asked.

"A million dollars to Me is like a penny to you," God replied.

"In that case," the young man ventured, "could I have one of Your pennies?"

"Certainly, My son," God replied. "Just a second."

☆ ☆ ☆

A little boy refused to eat the prunes his mother served for dessert. She insisted. He persisted. She even reminded him that God didn't like it when little boys didn't obey their mothers. Nothing worked. So she sent him to his room.

During the evening, a storm arose. She wondered how her son might be doing alone in his room, so she cautiously opened the door and peeked in. He was looking out at the raucous elements. A tear came to her eye and a smile to her lips when she heard him say: "My, my! Such a fuss over a few prunes."

Lee Trevino was asked for his thoughts the day he was struck by lightning on the golf course. "I learned," he said, "that when God wants to play through, you'd better let Him."

☆　☆　☆

Sadness was written all over Martin Luther's face one morning when he sat at the breakfast table with his wife. "What time is the funeral?" she asked.

"What funeral? Who died?" he wanted to know.

She said, "From the look on your face, I thought God had."

☆　☆　☆

In his search for a bird's nest, a man fell over a cliff, but saved himself by clinging to a branch. Not knowing how to get back up, he heard a voice that said, "I can help you. I am the Lord. Do you believe I can help you?"

The man answered, "Of course, I trust You completely."

"Then," said the Lord, "let go and I will take care of you." Silence. "Well, what do you say?" the Lord asked.

"I say," the man answered, "is there anybody else up there?"

SOME MESSAGES FROM GOD:

"Let's meet at my house Sunday before the game."
"C'mon over to my house and bring the kids."

"What part of 'thou shalt not' didn't you understand?"

"Loved the wedding, invite me to the marriage."

"You think it's hot *here?*"

"Tell the kids I love them."

"That 'love thy neighbor' thing? I mean it."

Golf

Returning home from a round of golf, a man was asked by his cheery wife, "Did you win today, honey?"

"Of course not," he muttered. "You know I was playing against the boss."

☆ ☆ ☆

"You think so much about your golf game that you don't even remember when we got married," complained the wife.

"Of course I do, honey," the husband protested. "It was the day after I sank that forty-foot putt."

☆ ☆ ☆

"Do you know what happens to little boys who use bad language when they're playing?" a mother asked her little son.

"Sure, Mom," he said. "They grow up and play golf."

In my hand I hold a ball
  White and dimpled, rather small
Oh, how harmless it does appear
  This innocent looking little sphere
By its size I could not guess
  The awesome power it does possess
But since I fell beneath its spell
  I've been through the fires of hell.
My life hasn't been quite the same
  Since I chose to play its game.
It rules my mind for hours on end
  A fortune it has had me spend
It has made me curse and cry
  And hate myself and want to die
It promises me a thing called "par"
  If I can hit it straight and far
To master such a tiny ball
  Should not be very hard at all
But my desires the ball refuses
  And does exactly as it chooses.
It hooks and slices, dribbles and dies
  or disappears before my eyes.
Often it will have a whim
  To hit a tree or take a swim
With miles of grass on which to land
  It finds that tiny patch of sand
Then has me offering up my soul
  If it would first drop in the hole
It's made me whimper like a pup
  And swear that I will give it up
And take to drink to ease my sorrow
  But the ball knows I'll be back tomorrow.

"Why don't you play golf with Frank anymore?" a wife asked her husband.

"Would you like to play with someone who cheats, gets mad, and uses foul language?" he replied.

"No, of course not," she said.

"Well, neither does Frank."

✩ ✩ ✩

A young man who was an avid golfer found himself with a few hours to spare one afternoon. He figured that if he played quickly, he could get in nine holes before he had to head home. Just as he was about to tee off, an old gentleman shuffled onto the tee and asked if he could play along. Not being able to say no, he allowed the old gent to join him.

To his surprise, the old man played fairly quickly. He didn't hit the ball far, but he plodded along consistently and didn't waste much time. Finally, they reached the ninth fairway and the young man found himself with a tough shot. There was large pine tree directly in front of him, and between his ball and the green. After several minutes of watching the young man debate how to hit the shot, the old man finally said, "You know, when I was your age, I'd hit the ball right over that tree." With that challenge placed before him, the youngster swung hard, hit the ball up—and right smack into the top of the tree trunk. It thudded back to the ground not a foot from its original spot. The old man offered one more comment, "Of course, when I was your age, that pine tree was only three feet tall."

A golfing duffer cringed when his drive landed in an anthill. Choosing a sand wedge, he positioned himself and slashed at the half-buried ball. Sand and ants flew. The ball wasn't touched.

Again the novice braced and swung. Again the ant hill was devastated, but the ball lay unmoved.

Among the panic-stricken ant colony, one ant yelled to a buddy, "Follow me! That big white ball there seems to be a pretty safe place!"

☆ ☆ ☆

The country club pro was insufferable—good at the game, and glad to remind anyone he defeated. When one of the members had finally had enough, he bought a gorilla and trained it to play golf. He then organized a game between the pro and the gorilla, with the loser to cough up $1,000.

On the day of the match, the pro teed off on the first hole, a 575-yard par-5. He split the fairway some 270 yards out.

Then the gorilla lumbered up to the tee. He took a mighty swing, and everyone watching stood in awe as the ball disappeared into the sky. By the time it landed, it was only five inches from the cup.

The pro knew he was in trouble. If this was an indication of the way things were going to go, he would never live it down. He immediately settled the bet, saying he had just remembered some urgent business across town.

As the group walked from the tee, the pro asked, "So how does he putt?"

The gorilla's manager replied with a grin, "The same as he drives—575 yards."

A man went in to the confessional and began, "Forgive me, Father, for I have sinned."

"What is your sin, my son?" the priest asked.

"Well, I used some horrible language this week and I feel absolutely terrible."

"When did you use this awful language?" asked the priest.

"I was golfing and hit an incredible drive that looked like it was going to go more than 250 yards, but it struck a phone line that was hanging over the fairway and fell straight down to the ground after going only about 110 yards."

"Is that when you swore?" the priest asked.

"No, Father," said the man. "After that, a squirrel ran out of the bushes and grabbed my ball in his mouth and began to run away."

"Is THAT when you swore?"

"Well, no," said the man. "You see, as the squirrel was running, an eagle came down out of the sky, grabbed it in his talons and began to fly away."

"Is THAT when you swore?" asked the priest, amazed.

"No, not yet," the man replied. "As the eagle carried the squirrel away in his claws, it flew toward the green. And as it passed over a bit of forest near the green, the squirrel dropped my ball."

"So that's when you swore?" asked the now impatient priest.

"No, because when the ball fell, it struck a tree, bounced through some bushes, careened off a big rock, and rolled through a sand trap onto the green and stopped within six inches of the hole."

The priest sighed, "You missed the putt, didn't you?"

☆ ☆ ☆

A retiring businessman was given a set of golf clubs by his co-workers. The following morning, he drove to the golf course and asked the local pro for lessons, explaining that he knew nothing whatever of the game.

The pro showed him the stance and swing, and then said, "Just hit the ball toward the flag on the first green."

The novice teed up the ball and smacked it straight down the fairway and onto the green, where it stopped inches from the hole.

"Now what?" the fellow asked the speechless pro.

After he was able to speak again, the pro said, "Uh. . . you're supposed to hit the ball into the cup."

"Oh great! NOW you tell me."

☆ ☆ ☆

Roger was just beginning to get over the tragedy of losing his golfing buddy, who'd dropped dead of a heart attack on the fairway some weeks earlier.

"It must have been terribly hard carrying him back to the clubhouse like you did," remarked a friend. "I understand he was a big man."

"Weighed about 230," Roger acknowledged. "And it was ninety degrees that day. Yeah, it was rough. Pick him up, find the ball, put him down, take my next shot. Pick him up, find the ball. . ."

There was this preacher who was an avid golfer. Every chance he could find, he was out on the golf course swinging away. It was an obsession.

He woke up one Sunday to find it was a picture perfect day for golf. The sun was shining in a cloudless sky, there was only the slightest breeze, and the temperature was just right. The preacher was in a quandary. Should he play golf or give the Sunday service?

Shortly, the urge to play golf overcame him. He called his associate pastor, told him he was sick, and asked the associate to take care of the Sunday church service for him. Then he packed his clubs and drove three hours to a golf course where no one would recognize him. Happily, he began to play the course, and he was having the round of his life. Every drive was long and true, his approaches were on the money, and his putting was the best it had ever been. At the turn, he was five strokes under par and ready to attack the back nine.

An angel up in heaven was watching the preacher and was quite perturbed. He went to God and said, "Look at that preacher. He should be punished for what he's doing." God nodded in agreement.

The preacher teed up on the tenth hole. He swung at

the ball and hit a perfect drive, straight as an arrow, four hundred yards right to the green, where it gently rolled into the cup. A picture perfect hole-in-one.

The preacher was amazed and excited, but the angel was shocked. He turned to God and said, "Begging your pardon, but I thought you were going to punish him."

God smiled and said, "I just did. Think about it. Whom can he tell?"

✩ ✩ ✩

Golf is a lot like business. You work hard to get to the green and then wind up in the hole.

✩ ✩ ✩

A man came to an infamous water hole on the course. He proceeded to pull out all the balls from his bag and throw them into the water. "What on earth are you doing?" he was asked.

"I'm saving time," he explained.

✩ ✩ ✩

A curious golfer asked his caddy, "Why do you keep looking at your watch?"

"It's not a watch," the caddy replied. "It's a compass."

Grab Bag

I once met an oil billionaire. When I asked him how he'd made so much money, he replied, "I just kept digging holes!"

☆ ☆ ☆

They have a Dial-A-Prayer for atheists. It rings and rings, but nobody answers.

☆ ☆ ☆

If at first you don't succeed, try again. Then quit. There's no reason to make a fool of yourself.

☆ ☆ ☆

Who was the greatest financier of all time?
   Noah. He floated stock while the rest of the world was in liquidation.

Every problem can be solved, except maybe how to refold a road map.

✫ ✫ ✫

Even a subway conductor shouldn't marry below his station.

✫ ✫ ✫

I just started on my second million. I gave up on the first!

✫ ✫ ✫

Why was King Solomon so wise?
  Because he had so many wives to advise him.

✫ ✫ ✫

Keep trying. Look at that man who put a hole in a Life Saver and made a mint!

✫ ✫ ✫

Who was the most sorry when the prodigal son returned?
  The fatted calf.

✫ ✫ ✫

What kind of lights did Noah have on the ark?
  Flood lights.

Whom was the first canning factory run by?
Noah—he had a boatful of preserved pairs.

☆ ☆ ☆

How do we know Abraham was smart?
He knew a Lot.

☆ ☆ ☆

Why couldn't Cain please God with his offering?
He just wasn't Abel.

☆ ☆ ☆

Who were the most famous triplets in the New Testament?
First, Second, and Third John.

☆ ☆ ☆

"Things are more like they are now than they ever were before." Dwight D. Eisenhower

☆ ☆ ☆

A husband is someone who takes out the trash and gives the impression that he just cleaned the whole house.

☆ ☆ ☆

A good way to save face is to keep the lower half shut.

"Traditionally, most of Australia's imports come from overseas." Australian Cabinet Minister Keppel Enderberry

☆ ☆ ☆

"I was most recently on a tour of Latin America, and the only regret I have is that I didn't study Latin harder in school so I could converse with these people." Dan Quayle

☆ ☆ ☆

Did you hear about the fellow from Los Angeles who passed out on a cruise ship?

They had to hold him over the smokestack to revive him.

☆ ☆ ☆

Silence is golden, because you never have to explain something you didn't say.

☆ ☆ ☆

The Concorde is great, but there is one problem. It travels twice the speed of sound, which is fun, but you can't hear the movie until two hours after you land.

☆ ☆ ☆

One guy I know had such a bad case of insomnia that the sheep fell asleep.

SOME ITEMS SEEN ON THE INTERNET:

Something Went Wrong in Jet Crash, Expert Says

War Dims Hope for Peace

Two Sisters Reunited After Eighteen Years in Checkout Counter

My mother is a travel agent for guilt trips.

If Strike Isn't Settled Quickly, It May Last a While

Local Couple Slain: Police Suspect Homicide

☆ ☆ ☆

A monastery in the English countryside had fallen on hard times, and decided to establish a business to defray their expenses. Being English, they decided to open a fish-and-chips restaurant. The establishment soon became very popular, attracting people from all over. One city fellow, thinking himself clever, asked one of the brothers standing nearby, "I suppose you're the 'fish friar'?"

"No," answered the brother levelly, "I'm the 'chip monk.'"

☆ ☆ ☆

I know the exact day I gave up jogging. It's on my birth certificate.

What did one toe say to another?
   Don't look now, but I think we're being followed by a heel.

☆ ☆ ☆

What did one wall say to the other?
   I'll meet you at the corner.

☆ ☆ ☆

What did one eye say to the other?
   I don't know what it is, but there's something between us that smells.

☆ ☆ ☆

For years, he thought he was a failure. Then he took a course in positive thinking.
   Now he's positive that he's a failure.

☆ ☆ ☆

I'd rather be a Could-Be
If I cannot be an Are;
Because a Could-Be is a May-Be
Who might be reaching for a star.
I'd rather be a Has-Been
Than a Might-Have-Been by far,
For a Might-Have-Been has never been
But a Has was once an Are!

A man was walking home alone one dark and foggy night when he heard an ominous sound behind him.

BUMP. . .BUMP. . .BUMP. . .

Walking faster, he looked back. Through the mist he could just make out the shape of an upright coffin banging its way down the middle of the street toward him.

BUMP. . .BUMP. . .BUMP. . .

Alarmed, the man began to run toward home, but the coffin bounced quickly after him—faster and faster.

BUMP. . .BUMP. . .BUMP. . .

Reaching his home, the man ran up to the door, fumbling with his keys. Finally, he opened the door, rushed inside, and locked the door behind himself.

He was reaching for the phone to diall 9-1-1, when the coffin came crashing through the front door. The lid of the coffin was clapping

BUMP. . .BUMP. . .BUMP. . .

Terrified now, the man rushed upstairs, into the bathroom, and locked the door. His heart was pounding and his breath was coming in ragged gasps.

CRASH!

The coffin broke down the door and began to squeeze its way into the bathroom. The man screamed and ripped open the medicine cabinet, looking for something—anything!—with which to defend himself. But all he could find was a box of cough drops!

Desperate, he threw the lozenges at the coffin. . . .

And, of course, the coffin stopped.

"When I was eighteen, the president of the United States honored me with a beauty award."

"Honestly? I didn't know Lincoln did that sort of thing!"

Grandparents

The grandparents were so thrilled to have their grand-children coming the next week that they threw an extra ten dollars in the offering plate on Sunday. The following Sunday, after the kids were gone, they put in an extra hundred.

☆　☆　☆

"Have I shown you the pictures of our new grandchild?" the proud grandmother asked a friend.

Her friend answered, "No, and I sure appreciate it."

☆　☆　☆

A grandson wrote his grandmother the following thank-you note:

"Dear Grandma, thanks for the sweater. I always wanted one, but not very much."

Her grandson was visiting and Grandma was doing everything to make him happy, including letting him eat all the pancakes he wanted. Finally after a goodly number, she asked, "How about some more?"

"No, thanks, Grandma," he replied. "I don't even want the ones I already had."

☆ ☆ ☆

When I stopped to pick up Chris for preschool, I saw an older woman hugging him as he left the house.

"Is that your grandmother?" I asked.

"Yes," Chris said. "She's come to visit us for Christmas."

"How nice," I said. "Where does she live?"

"At the airport," Chris replied. "Whenever we want her, we just go to the airport and get her."

☆ ☆ ☆

Little Boy: "Grandfather, make like a frog."
Grandfather: "What do you mean, make like a frog?"
Boy: "Croak. Daddy says we're going to have a lot of money when you croak."

187

A grandmother called her daughter's house and her grandson answered the phone, whispering, "Hello?"

Grandma: "Hello, Tommy, this is Grandma. Is your mother there?"

Tommy (whispering): "Yes, but she's busy."

Grandma: "How about your father? Is he there?"

Tommy (still whispering): "Yes, but he's busy too."

Grandma: "What's all that noise in the background?"

Tommy (whispering): "Those are policemen and firemen."

Grandma: "Goodness! What are they doing?"

Tommy (still whispering): "They're looking for me."

Grown-ups

When a precocious nine-year-old was asked by her teacher to write an essay on "Where My Family Came From," she decided to undertake a bit of research. So, before supper, she sat at the table where she often did her homework and asked her mother some questions.

"Mom, where did I come from?"

Her mother, being a bit old-fashioned, found herself saying, "Well, the stork brought you, dear."

"Where did you come from, then?"

"Uh, the stork brought me, too."

"Okay, then where did Granny come from?"

"The stork brought her, too, dear."

"Okay, thanks, Mom," said the girl, who settled down to writing her assignment. After about five minutes, the mother happened to walk by her daughter and read the first sentence of the essay: "For three generations, there have been no natural births in our family."

"Dad, which do you think is America's worst problem: ignorance or apathy?"

"Don't know. Don't really care, either."

☆ ☆ ☆

A five-year-old came into the kitchen and asked, "Mommy, can I have a slice of strawberry pie?"

"Now, Randall," his mother corrected, "you don't say 'can I have.' You say 'may I have.' "

"Okay. May I have a slice of strawberry pie?"

"And what do you say at the end?"

"Oh—may I have a slice of strawberry pie, please?"

"No, dear. We'll be having dinner in less than an hour."

☆ ☆ ☆

"Mom, why do you put on all that makeup before you go to bed?" a child asked, watching her mother apply the nightly ritual.

"It's not really makeup," her mother explained. "It's mostly a variety of creams to protect my skin and make me feel better after a long day. This one is for wrinkles, for example. And this hand lotion is great for my joints. And this facial cream gives me a healthy, pink color."

"I'm surprised they don't leave you black and blue all over."

"Why do you say that?"

"They make you so greasy, you must slip out of bed a lot and fall on the floor."

"But I don't wanna help Billy with his homework," Father complained to Mother. "It's boring, and he shouldn't need help, anyway. He's simply not thinking for himself. He's getting someone else to do his thinking for him."

"Now, Honey, you go in there and help him while you can," Mother replied. "You know he'll soon be a third-grader."

☆ ☆ ☆

A little girl was sitting at the kitchen table one day, watching her mother do the dishes at the sink, when she suddenly noticed that her mother had several strands of white sticking out in contrast to her otherwise brunette hair. Looking at her mother inquisitively, she asked, "Mommy, why are some of your hairs white?"

Her mother replied, "Well, every time that you do something wrong and make me cry or unhappy, one of my hairs turns white."

The little girl thought about this revelation for a while, and then said, "Wow, you must have been a naughty little girl, Mommy, because *all* of Grandma's hairs are white!"

A salesman telephoned a household, and a four-year-old boy answered:

Salesman: "May I speak to your mother?"

Boy: "She's not here."

Salesman: "Well, is anyone else there?"

Boy: "My sister."

Salesman: "Okay, fine. May I speak to her?"

Boy: "I guess so."

A lengthy silence ensued. At last, the boy came back on the phone.

Boy: "Hello?"

Salesman: "It's you. I thought you were going to let me talk to your sister."

Boy: "I was, but I can't get her out of the playpen."

☆　☆　☆

"Mom, Dad just hit his thumb with a hammer."

"Oh, dear. What did he say?"

"You wouldn't want me to repeat any bad words, would you, Mom?"

"Certainly not."

"Well, then, he didn't say anything."

"Dad, there's something I've gotta tell you," Shane said, following his father inside the bait shop.

"Not, now, son. I have to select our fish bait."

Later, entering the convenience store, Shane tried again. "Hey, Dad—"

"Hold on, son. I have to grab some lunch for our fishing trip."

At the gas station, dad was filling the boat tank when Shane began, "Dad, there's something you really need to know. . . ."

"Just wait, son. I need to pay for this gas so we can hit the road."

An hour later, as they sat on the pond bank catching fish, the father remembered his son's nagging. "What was it you were trying to tell me awhile ago?" he asked.

"Oh, not much. Just that your fly is open."

Headlines

Include your Children when Baking Cookies

Police Begin Campaign to Run Down Jaywalkers

Safety Experts Say School Bus Passengers Should
Be Belted

Drunk Gets Nine Months in Violin Case

Survivor of Siamese Twins Joins Parents

Farmer Bill Dies in House

Iraqi Head Seeks Arms

British Left Waffles on Falkland Islands

Lung Cancer in Women Mushrooms

Eye Drops off Shelf

Teacher Strikes Idle Kids

Squad Helps Dog Bite Victim

Enraged Cow Injures Farmer with Ax

Plane Too Close to Ground, Crash Probe Told

Miners Refuse to Work after Death

Juvenile Court to Try Shooting Defendant

Two Soviet Ships Collide, One Dies

Killer Sentenced to Die for Second Time in 10 Years

Cold Wave Linked to Temperatures

Enfields Couple Slain; Police Suspect Homicide

Red Tape Holds Up New Bridge

Deer Kill 17,000

Typhoon Rips Through Cemetery; Hundreds Dead

Man Struck by Lightning Faces Battery Charge

New Study of Obesity Looks for Larger Test Group

Kids Make Nutritious Snacks

Chef Throws His Heart into Helping Feed Needy

Arson Suspect is Held in Massachusetts Fire

British Union Finds Dwarfs in Short Supply

Lansing Residents Can Drop Off Trees

Local High School Dropouts Cut in Half

New Vaccine May Contain Rabies

Deaf College Opens Doors to Hearing

Air Head Fired

Steals Clock, Faces Time

Old School Pillars are Replaced by Alumni

Bank Drive-in Window Blocked by Board

Hospitals are Sued by 7 Foot Doctors

Health

Before the latest developments in open heart surgery, heart valves were sometimes replaced with a metal ball that could be heard working. "Doesn't that bother you, hearing that click, click, click all day?" a man with a new valve was asked.

He replied, "It's a lot better than not hearing it!"

☆ ☆ ☆

"Give it to me straight, Doctor. I can take it," a man said to his physician.

"Let me put it this way," the doctor answered. "If I were you, I wouldn't buy any green bananas."

Billie Burke found herself seated on a plane with a man who was struggling with a head cold. She proceeded to advise him about taking care of it. "Drink lots of water, go to bed, do this, do that," she went on, and then added: "Now do what I said; I know what I'm talking about—I'm Billie Burke of Hollywood."

The man thanked her and then introduced himself: "And I'm Dr. Mayo of the Mayo Clinic."

☆ ☆ ☆

A man was seen fleeing down the hall of the hospital just before his operation. "What's the matter?" he was asked.

He said, "I heard the nurse say, 'It's a very simple operation, don't worry, I'm sure it will be all right.'"

"She was just trying to comfort you. What's so frightening about that?"

"She wasn't talking to me. She was talking to the doctor."

☆ ☆ ☆

George Burns writes about his heart bypass operation. He decided he wouldn't worry, because it was out of his hands. It was the doctor's responsibility. After the operation, the doctor complimented him on his composure. "George, you did just great."

"Doctor," Burns said, "I wasn't the least bit concerned."

"Really?" the doctor asked. "I was a nervous wreck."

"Even that didn't bother me," Burns writes, "but then the doctor gave me his bill and I fainted."

Anybody who can swallow an aspirin at a drinking fountain deserves to get well.

☆　☆　☆

"Do you suffer from arthritis?"

"Of course, what else can you do with it?"

☆　☆　☆

A woman was suffering from depression, so her concerned husband took her to a psychiatrist. The doctor listened to their story and then said, "The treatment I prescribe is really quite simple." With that, he went over to the man's wife, gathered her up in his arms, and gave her a big kiss. He then stepped back and looked at the woman's glowing face and broad smile. She looked better already. Turning to her husband, he said, "See, that's all she needs to put new sparkle back in her."

The husband said, "Okay, Doc. I can bring her in on Tuesdays and Thursdays."

☆　☆　☆

Hypochondria is the only disease I haven't got.

☆　☆　☆

In his book, *How to Live to be 100,* George Burns writes that when you get to be one hundred, you've got it made, because very few people die at such an old age.

Heaven

St. Peter was happily walking around near the Pearly Gates when he heard a funny little sound and saw a lot of little things scurrying about. When he realized that heaven had a new delegation of mice, he asked them, "How do you like it up here?"

They replied, "Well, the accommodations are superb, but we have a complaint. Heaven is so large, and our legs are so short that it's hard for us to get around and see everything."

"Not to worry," St. Peter assured them and promptly ordered roller skates for all the mice. The next day, the mice were darting all over, having a whale of a time. A week later, Peter went for his stroll and—no mice. He looked around but couldn't find them. All of a sudden, he came upon a fat and happy old cat that was sleeping in the corner. He said, "Well, cat, how are you doing? How do you like heaven?"

And the cat said, "It's paradise. It's clean, it's quiet, the weather is nice, and those meals on wheels are terrific."

"Mom, are there animals in heaven?"

"What kinds of animals?"

"Regular animals, like cows and bees."

"I'm not sure about that. I doubt they'll be necessary in heaven."

"Then where are we going to get enough milk and honey for everybody?"

✫ ✫ ✫

A man's most memorable experience was the famous Johnstown flood. He never stopped talking about it. When he died and went to heaven, he asked if he could tell the people about his experiences. St. Peter told him he thought it could be arranged. "But you must remember," he cautioned the man, "that Noah will be in the audience."

✫ ✫ ✫

A grumbling man got to heaven with his wife, but even there he seemed dissatisfied. "What's the matter with you?" his wife asked. "Here we are in Paradise. Everything is perfect. We've never had such delicious food. Our mansion is beautiful. The golf course is finer than any we've ever seen. There are no dues, no taxes. Our health is perfect. I just can't believe you're not happy. What is wrong?"

He explained, "If you hadn't made me eat that miserable oat bran, we could have been here ten years ago."

A husband said to his wife, "I'm not so sure you can't take it with you. I'm going to put a few thousand dollars in the attic and when we go we can pick it up on our way to heaven."

When the husband later died, his wife went up to the attic to see how his plan had worked. The money was still there. As she went back downstairs she mused, "Maybe he should have put it in the basement."

☆ ☆ ☆

A Sunday school teacher asked her class, "How many of you want to go to heaven?"

They all raised their hands, except one little girl.

After class, the teacher asked her, "Why didn't you raise your hand?"

She replied, "I want to go to heaven, but my mother said I have to go straight home after Sunday school."

☆ ☆ ☆

While handing a manufacturer's coupon to the clerk at the supermarket checkout counter, a woman accidentally missed her hand, and the coupon slipped beneath the conveyor belt and was gone.

The clerk looked upset, so the woman said, "That's all right. It's in coupon heaven now."

"Coupon heaven?" the checker asked.

"Yes," the woman replied. "That's where coupons go when they die."

"Only the redeemed ones!" the clerk corrected.

One person's nightmare: Standing in line where the credentials for heaven are being checked, finding yourself behind Mother Teresa and then hearing the Lord say, "You really could have done a little better."

☆ ☆ ☆

A rich man was near death, and feeling sorry for himself because he had worked so hard for his money and wanted badly to take it with him to heaven. So he began to pray that he might be able to carry his wealth with him. Before long, an angel appeared, saying, "Sorry, but you can't take your wealth with you."

The man implored the angel to speak to God to see if He might bend the rules. The man continued to pray that he could take his money with him to heaven. After a time, the angel reappeared and told the man that God would let him take one suitcase with him. Overjoyed, the man gathered his largest piece of luggage and filled it with pure gold bars, placing it beside his bed.

Soon afterward the man died. When he appeared at the Gates of Heaven, St. Peter, noticing the suitcase said, "Hold on—you can't bring that in here!" But the man explained to St. Peter that he had a special permission from the Lord. St. Peter checked out the man's story, and came back saying, "All right. You're allowed one carry-on bag, but I'm supposed to check its contents before letting it through."

St. Peter opened the suitcase to inspect the worldly items that the man found too precious to leave behind and exclaimed, "You brought pavement?"

Hillbillies

"I hear old Ebenezer Todd died the other day up in Jonesville," said an old timer, playing checkers at the country store.

"Yeah, they say he died of a head injury."

"Head injury? It must've taken a powerful wallop to do in that tough old coot."

"No, wasn't much more'n a scratch, from what I hear. In fact, he was startin' to come around, but then his wife came along and tied a tourniquet around his neck."

✩ ✩ ✩

Ma: "I think Adam and Eve must have been hillbillies, just like us."

Pa: "What makes you say that?"

Ma: "Didn't have a fancy house. Didn't drive a car. Didn't go to college. Didn't have any money— but as far as they were concerned, life was just like paradise."

A salesman was trying to strike up a conversation with a wily, tight-lipped mountaineer. "Have you lived all your life in these parts?" he tried.

"Not yet," was the sour reply.

☆ ★ ☆

In the hills of Appalachia, a man attending the Sunday morning service heard the story of Jesus' turning water into wine.

On his way home, the man was stopped at a road-block, where the sher-iff was checking cars for moonshine, because a new still had recently opened in the area. The sheriff looked under the tarp on the back of the man's pickup and saw a number of corked crocks.

"What do you have in those?" the sheriff asked.

"Spring water," the man replied. "My wife and I drink only spring water."

The sheriff poured a little of the fluid and drank it. "That's whiskey," he declared.

"It is?" the man asked. "Well, praise the Lord, He's done it again."

The city woman was driving a secondary route through the mountains at night. She hadn't seen a town for miles, and her gas gauge was almost on empty. Finally, she came to a crossroads community with a few houses. A ramshackle country store had a light on and a single, antiquated gas pump in front. Happily, the storekeeper assured her that the pump still worked.

"This sure is a tiny village," the woman said as he topped off her tank. "What on earth do you do for a living around here?"

"We charge $10 a gallon for gas," he drawled.

☆ ☆ ☆

A stranger walked inside the community store at a remote village. "Where's the movie theater?" he asked.

"We don't have one," the clerk replied.

"What about a golf course?"

"We don't play golf."

"Well, where's your local baseball diamond. Surely you have baseball."

"Nope."

"Then what do you do for fun around here. Where do you people play video games?"

"Same place we play baseball and golf and watch movies."

History

"Who invented the bow and arrow?" asked the teacher.

"Cavemen!" cried Gary enthusiastically.

"Cavemen? And what do you suppose prompted cavemen to come up with the bow and arrow?"

"Er. . .somebody kept stealing the wheel?"

☆ ☆ ☆

"What was the principal occupation of the ancient Babylonians?" a college history student was asked.

"Dying, I believe."

☆ ☆ ☆

"What do you think was the most important invention in all of history?" the teacher asked his class.

"The automobile," said one student.

"The airplane," said another.

"The nuclear submarine," said the third.

"The credit card," said the fourth.

History Teacher: "Who was the most famous Egyptian in history?"
Student: "The Mummy."

✫ ✫ ✫

"Can you give us an example of an absolute monarchy?" the teacher asked.

"France, during the colonial period."

"And we know that absolute monarchies present lots of difficulties for the common people, don't we?"

"Yeah, but they sure are cool for the monarch."

History Revisited

Here are some answers turned in by students on a history exam:

✪ ✪ ✪

"David was a Hebrew king skilled at playing the liar. Solomon, his son, had three hundred wives and five hundred porcupines."

✪ ✪ ✪

"A great writer was John Milton. He wrote *Paradise Lost.* Then his wife died and he wrote *Paradise Regained.*"

✪ ✪ ✪

"The Romans were called Romans because they never stayed in one place very long. Nero was a cruel tyrant who tortured his subjects by playing the fiddle."

"The First World War was caused by the assignation of the Arch-Duck by a surf. This ushered in a new error in the annals of human history."

☆ ☆ ☆

"Without the Greeks, we wouldn't have history. Socrates died from an overdose of wedlock. The Greeks invented the Olympic Games, where they hurled biscuits and threw the java."

☆ ☆ ☆

"Then came the Middle Ages, when King Alfred conquered the Dames and the Magna Carta proved that no free man should be hanged twice for the same crime."

☆ ☆ ☆

"The government of England was a limited mockery. Henry VIII found walking difficult because he had an abbess on his knees. Queen Elizabeth was the Virgin Queen. When she exposed herself before the troops, they all shouted, 'Hurray!' Then her navy went out and defeated the Spanish Armadillo."

☆ ☆ ☆

"Meanwhile, in Europe, gravity was invented by Isaac Walton. It is chiefly noticeable in the autumn when the apples are falling."

"Queen Victoria was the longest queen. She sat on a thorn for sixty-three years."

☆   ☆   ☆

"Christopher Columbus discovered America while cursing the Atlantic. When the Pilgrims landed, they were greeted by Indians, who came down the hill rolling their war hoops before them and carrying their porpoises on their back. Many were killed along with their cabooses. Many died during the hard winter but the next spring many babies were born. Captain John Smith was responsible for this."

☆   ☆   ☆

"The Renaissance was the time when Martin Luther was nailed to the church door. He died a horrible death, being excommunicated by a papal bull. Gutenberg invented the Bible and Sir Walter Raleigh invented pipe tobacco."

Holidays

A Russian couple was walking down a Moscow street one night, when the man felt a drop hit his nose. "I think it's raining," he said to his wife.

"No, I think that would be snow," she replied.

"Look, I'm sure it was rain," he said. The couple was about to begin a full-scale argument when they noticed a minor communist party official walking toward them.

"Let's not fight about it," the man suggested. "Let's ask Comrade Rudolph whether it's officially raining or snowing."

As the official came near, the man said, "Tell us, Comrade Rudolph, is it officially raining or snowing?"

"It's raining, of course," he replied, and walked on.

But the woman insisted: "I'm sure that was snow!"

The man quietly replied: "Rudolph the Red knows rain, dear!"

Thanksgiving Day was approaching and the family had received a card with a painting of a Pilgrim family on their way to church. Grandma showed the card to her small grandchildren, observing: "The Pilgrim children liked to go to church with their mothers and fathers."

"Oh yeah?" her young grandson replied. "So why is their dad carrying that rifle?"

☆ ☆ ☆

After turning ninety, Marie found that shopping for Christmas gifts had become too difficult, so she decided to send checks to everyone instead. She wrote "Buy your own present" on each card and mailed them early.

Marie enjoyed the usual flurry of family festivities. Only after Christmas did she get around to clearing off her cluttered desk. Under a stack of papers, she was horrified to find the gift checks, which she had forgotten to enclose.

☆ ☆ ☆

It was Memorial Day weekend, and the church was filled with patriotic decorations. Little Tommy, sitting with his grandfather, was particularly impressed with the row of small U.S. flags on the edge of the platform.

"Grandpa," he asked, "what are all those flags for?"

"Well, Tommy," his grandfather replied, "they honor the boys who died in the service."

Tommy was taken aback. "Which one—morning or evening?"

Did you hear about the department store that had two Santas? One for regular kids and one for kids who wanted ten toys or less.

☆　☆　☆

Just before the Thanksgiving holiday, the teacher asked her kindergarten class, "What do you have to be thankful for?"

One youngster answered, "I'm thankful I'm not a turkey!"

Honesty

"I'm moving out," one renter said. "But first, I'm getting a thousand roaches. The agreement states I should leave the place the way I found it."

✩ ✩ ✩

One day, the captain wrote in the log, "First mate drunk today."

When the first mate found out, he was upset and said to the captain, "It is true that I had too much to drink. But Captain," he pleaded, "remember that this has never happened before and it will never happen again. It was my day off, I had just heard that I was a father of my first child, and I guess we celebrated a little too much."

The captain, however, was unmoved and told him, "That may all be true, but it is still a fact. You were drunk that day, and so we will just let it stand." Without another word, the first mate went on duty, but the next morning when the captain looked at the log, he read, "Captain sober today."

A teacher observed a boy entering the classroom with filthy hands. She stopped him and said, "John, please wash your hands. My goodness, what would you say if I came into the room with hands like that?"

With a smile the boy replied, "I think I'd be too polite to mention it."

☆ ☆ ☆

After the church service, a little boy told the pastor, "When I grow up, I'm going to give you some money."

"Well, thank you," the pastor replied. "But why?"

"Because Daddy says you're one of the poorest preachers we've ever had."

☆ ☆ ☆

There were two evil brothers. They were rich and used their money to hide their evil ways. One day, one of the brothers died. The remaining brother talked to the pastor about the funeral. "I have here a check for the full amount to pay for a new building. I have only one condition: At my brother's funeral, you must say he was a saint."

The pastor knew all about the evil ways of these brothers. How could he call one of them a saint? he wondered. Nevertheless, he accepted the check and promised to say that the deceased was a saint.

The next day at the funeral, the pastor did not hold back. "He was an evil man," he said, and spelled out some of the man's evil ways. Then he concluded by saying, "But, compared to his brother, he was a saint."

The farmer's wife sold her surplus butter to a grocer. On one occasion, the grocer told her, "Your butter was underweight last week."

She replied, "That's interesting. My scale was broken so I used the pound of sugar you sold me to measure my butter."

☆ ☆ ☆

"Did you thank the lady for the party?" a mother asked her son.

He replied, "Well, I was going to, but a girl ahead of me said, 'Thank you,' and the lady told her not to mention it. So I didn't."

☆ ☆ ☆

My wife invited some people to dinner. At the table, she asked her six-year-old daughter, "Would you like to say the blessing?"

The girl replied, "I wouldn't know what to say."

"Just say what you've heard me say," Mommy said.

So the little one bowed her head and prayed, "Lord, why on earth did I invite all these people to dinner?"

Human Nature

Gizmo: "Are you superstitious?"
Dave: "Shhhhh! It's bad luck to be superstitious."

☆ ☆ ☆

"You just don't know who to trust these days," said Mick. "I put a dollar in a vending machine, and it gave me back a Canadian quarter for change."

"That's too bad," said Nick. "A lot of businesses won't accept those."

"I know. I got rid of it, though."

"How?"

"Left it as a tip at the coffee shop."

☆ ☆ ☆

Mick: "Can you keep a secret?"
Rick: "Sure. Of course, I can't vouch for the people I tell it to."

Harold: "My mom said it's only a coincidence that you and I have the same last name, because we're not related. Do you know what the word 'coincidence' means?"

George: "Nah, I was about to ask you what it means."

✰ ✰ ✰

Three mice lugged their prize of cheese out to the shade tree to enjoy a picnic lunch. Suddenly, a dark cloud came up and it began raining heavily.

"We need an umbrella," said one. "Who's going back to the house to get it?"

Each mouse was afraid that if it left the picnic, the other two would eat all the cheese. Finally, they resolved the question by drawing straws. The loser hesitantly disappeared into the driving rain.

The two other mice eyed the cheese hungrily. But being honest critters, they refrained from indulging before their friend returned with the umbrella.

The third mouse was gone for ten minutes. Then thirty minutes. Then an hour.

"Something's happened," said one of the waiting mice. "I don't think our friend's coming back today. We may as well dig into the cheese."

"I agree," said the other.

Just then the third mouse squeaked from behind the tree, "Touch that cheese, and I won't go for the umbrella!"

"Old Mr. Clancy sure is grumpy."

"What makes you think so?"

"If you pay him a compliment, he doesn't trust you. If you don't pay him a compliment, he doesn't like you at all."

☆　☆　☆

Mother: "Jack, you're always procrastinating. You must change."

Jack: "Sure, Mom. I'll change, I promise. I'll start Monday."

☆　☆　☆

We have thirty-five million laws to enforce the Ten Commandments.

Hunting

An avid duck hunter was looking for a new bird dog. When he found a dog that could actually walk on water to retrieve a duck, he knew his search was over. He knew none of his friends would ever believe in his new dog's abilities, so he decided to break the news to a cynical friend of his by taking the man hunting.

At the shore of the lake, a flock of ducks flew by. They fired, and one duck fell. The dog responded by jumping into the water. He proudly trotted across the lake to retrieve the bird, never getting more than his paws wet.

The cynical friend watched the display, but said nothing.

On the drive home the hunter asked his friend, "Did you notice anything unusual about my new dog?"

"Sure," said the friend. "He can't swim."

Two easterners were hunting in the Rocky Mountain wilderness when a huge grizzly bear sprang onto their path, reared up and roared.

One hunter was paralyzed with fright. The other kept his presence of mind and advised calmly, "Don't move a muscle. Just stand like a statue, and the bear will get bored and go away."

"H–h–how do you know?"

"Read it in a book about the Lewis and Clark expedition."

So they stood motionless. The bear didn't go away, but instead drew closer and roared more furiously.

"I–I–I think the bear must've read that same book!" stammered the frightened hunter.

☆　☆　☆

"Any luck hunting?"

"I shot fifteen ducks."

"Were they wild?"

"No, but the farmer who owned them was!"

☆　☆　☆

Paul: "Willie finally shot his first wild duck this morning."

Brad: "Reckon it won't be worth cookin'."

Paul: "Why not?"

Brad: "Must've been a very old duck, if it was flyin' low enough for Willie to shoot it."

Early one morning Ted, an avid hunter, woke up ready to bag the first deer of the season. As he entered the kitchen for breakfast, he was surprised to find his wife, Debbie, sitting there, fully dressed in hunter's camouflage.

"What are you doing?" Ted asked.

Debbie smiled. "I'm going hunting with you!"

Ted reluctantly decided to take Debbie along. Upon arriving at the hunting site, Ted set Debbie up in the tree stand and said: "If you see a deer, take careful aim and fire. I'll come running back as soon as I hear the shot."

Ted walked away expecting not a sound from Debbie's stand. But within ten minutes he was startled to hear an array of gunshots. As Jake ran back to Debbie's location, he heard her yelling: "Get away from my deer!"

Confused, Ted ran even faster toward his screaming wife. Again he heard her yell: "Get away from my deer!" Then Debbie let loose with another volley of gunfire.

Coming into sight of Debbie's stand, Ted was shocked to see a cowboy, with his hands held high in the air. The distraught cowboy, trying to defuse the situation, said: "Okay, lady, okay! You can have your deer! Just let me get my saddle off it!"

☆ ☆ ☆

A man attired in camouflage entered a butcher shop. "Can you sell me a couple of undressed ducks?" he asked.

"Well, no. We have no fresh ducks at the moment. I can sell you a nice selection of poultry broilers, though."

"Chickens!" the customer scoffed. "No way. I can't go home and tell my wife I bagged a couple of chickens!"

Four hunters were bragging about the merits of their favorite blue tick hounds.

"My ol' Benny goes to the store for me," said one. "Always brings me back my favorite brand of tobacco."

"My dog Suzie buys our grits at that same store," said another. "I give her a five-dollar bill, and she brings me back the change first, then returns for the bag of grits."

"I send ol' Mack there for my shotgun shells," said the third. "He knows exactly what gauge and brand I want."

The fourth hunter said nothing until he was prompted by the others to try to top their tales.

"I reckon my dog ain't much to speak of, by comparison," he allowed. "He just sits in the store all day and operates the cash register."

Husbands and Wives

A woman who was trying on a floor-length mink coat admired herself in it, and said to the clerk, "If my husband doesn't like it, will you promise me that you'll refuse to take it back?"

☆ ☆ ☆

A father was showing pictures of his wedding to his young son. The boy asked, "Is that when mother came to work for us?"

☆ ☆ ☆

A woman showed her friend a magnificent diamond in a platinum setting, and explained, "My husband died last month, but just before he breathed his last, he told me about some money set aside in a bank vault. He told me to buy a stone with it. This is the stone!"

A couple walking along the street stopped to look in the window of a famous jewelry store. The woman said, "I'd love that little diamond pin right there."

The man took a brick out of his pocket, tossed it through the window and handed her the pin.

They walked on and soon came to another jewelry store, where the woman saw a pair of diamond earrings that she liked. Her husband pulled out another brick, tossed it through the glass, and handed his wife the earrings.

The couple walked on until they arrived outside a third jewelry store. Looking in the window, the woman said, "Oh, I'd love to have that diamond ring."

"What is this with you?" her husband spouted. "You must think I'm made of bricks!"

☆　☆　☆

Husband: "I find your new evening gown rather confusing."
Wife: "How so?"
Husband: "Well, are you inside trying to get out, or outside trying to get in?"

☆　☆　☆

The new widow requested the epitaph "Rest in Peace" for her husband's tombstone. When she later found out he'd left her nothing in his will, she attempted to change her congenial words, but the tombstone had already been chiseled and could not be changed. "In that case," she told the engraver, "please add, 'Till we meet again.' "

A reporter once asked Winston Churchill after an election in which he had retained his seat in Parliament, "I presume we may expect you to continue to be subservient to the powerful interests that control your vote."

To which Churchill replied, "I'll thank you to keep my wife out of this."

✩　✩　✩

Two men were overheard in line at the local coffee establishment bragging about how much control they had over their wives. A third man was listening but remained quiet. After a while, the two men turned to the third and said, "Well, what about you? Does your wife know who's boss in your family?"

The third fellow smiled and said, "I'll tell you. Just the other night my wife came to me on her hands and knees."

The first two blokes where amazed. "What happened then?" they asked.

"She said, 'Get out from under the bed and fight like a man!' "

✩　✩　✩

"My wife never stops asking for money," a man complained to a friend. "Last week it was a hundred dollars, the week before fifty, now she wants two hundred."

"What does she do with all that money?" his friend asked.

"I don't know," he answered, "I never give her any."

As Alicia was getting to know Michael and his family, she was very impressed by how much his parents loved each other. "They're so thoughtful," Alicia said, "Why, your dad even brings your mom a cup of hot coffee in bed every morning."

After a time, Alicia and Michael were engaged, and then married. On the way from the wedding to the reception, Alicia again remarked on Michael's loving parents, and even the coffee in bed. "Tell me," she said, "does it run in the family?"

"It sure does," replied Michael, "and I take after my mom."

☆　☆　☆

On the way home from church, the pastor's wife said to him, "Darling, did anyone ever tell you that you're the greatest preacher in the world?"

"No," he said, his chest swelling with pride. "They never did."

"So, tell me," she said, "wherever did you get the idea?"

☆　☆　☆

A man looked up from his hospital bed and said to his wife: "You've always been with me in times of trouble. When I lost my shirt in a poor investment, you were there. When I had the car accident, you were with me. I got fired, and you were there. I've come to the conclusion," he told her, "that you must be bad luck."

A husband and wife were having a quarrel over the breakfast table. The quarrel remained unresolved when it was time to leave for work. The wife, having trouble with the zipper on her dress, asked for his assistance. In a huff, the husband freed the zipper and then angrily ran it up and down rapidly several times.

That afternoon, when the wife returned from work, she saw him lying on his back with his hands and head under the car working on it. Still smarting from what he had done that morning she went over, grasped his zipper and yanked it up and down several times and stomped into the house. There, to her great surprise, sat her husband drinking a cup of coffee. In great embarrassment, she explained to her husband what she had done. He rushed outside to find his neighbor, who had offered to fix his car, out cold. When the wife had grasped his zipper, he had reflexively tried to sit up and knocked himself out on the frame of the car.

☆ ☆ ☆

My wife wanted to see my paycheck go farther, so she took it to Paris!

☆ ☆ ☆

"Does your husband believe in life after death?" a minister asked a woman. When she started to laugh he asked her what was so amusing.

She told him: "You asked if he believes in life after death—why, he doesn't even believe in life after supper!"

A woman wore a huge emerald pendant to the great charity event of the season. All the women crowded around her to get a closer look at the glistening gem. The woman boasted, "This happens to be the third largest emerald in the whole world. The largest belongs to the Queen of England. Then comes the Onassis. Then comes this one, which is called the Robertson."

"What a jewel!" How lucky you are!"

"Wait, nothing in life is that easy," said the woman. "Unfortunately, the wearer of this fabulous emerald must bear with the famous Robertson curse."

The ladies were silent for but a second. "And what is the Robertson curse?"

The woman sighed, "Mr. Robertson."

☆ ☆ ☆

New Bride: "My husband is very good to me. He gives me everything I ask for."

Her Mother: "That only shows you're not asking for enough."

☆ ☆ ☆

Jake was on his deathbed. His wife, Becky, was at his side. With tears streaming down his face, he said, "Becky, I must confess. . ."

Becky interupted, "Hush. Don't try to talk."

Jake said, "No, I want a clean conscience. I must confess I've been unfaithful to you."

Becky replied, "Yes, I know. Why else would I have poisoned you?"

A young man leaving his village in Ireland to study theology in Rome visited friends to say good-bye and see if there was anything he could do for them in Rome.

"Well, yes," they said, "we've always wanted children. Please light a candle for us in Rome."

The young man was gone for many years. When he got back, he went to see his friends again and found, to his happy surprise, the father with a house full of children. "This is wonderful," the priest said, "but where is your wife?"

His friend answered, "Oh, she's gone to Rome to blow out the candle."

☆ ☆ ☆

In days past, children were given names that sound strange to us today—Prudence, Charity, Faith, and so on. One boy was named Amazing and he resented it all his life. People laughed at him because of it. He told his wife that, when the time came, he did not want his name on his tombstone. When he died, she followed his wishes and put on the tombstone, "Here lies a man who was faithful to his wife for sixty years."

But even in death he couldn't escape the curse, because everyone who looked at his tombstone said, "Why, that's amazing."

☆ ☆ ☆

My wife thinks I'm too nosy. At least that's what she keeps writing in her diary.

One aspect of marriage was well explained by a girl who wrote the following biography for a school assignment: "Benjamin Franklin was born in Boston, and moved to Philadelphia. He got married and discovered electricity."

☆　☆　☆

A minister was looking into the spiritual condition of one of his parishioners. When he asked her how things were going, she replied, "The old devil is still giving me trouble."

At that, her husband spoke up and said, "Now wait a minute; you're not so easy to live with yourself."

☆　☆　☆

While on a car trip, an elderly couple stopped at a road-side restaurant for lunch. After finishing their meal, the woman left her glasses on the table, but she didn't miss them until the car was back on the highway. By then, they had to travel quite a distance before they could find a place to turn around. The old man fussed and complained all the way back to the restaurant, criticizing his wife for being careless and chiding her for her forgetfulness. When they finally arrived at the restaurant, as the woman was getting out of the car to retrieve her glasses, her husband groused, "While you're in there, you might as well get my hat, too."

Stanley and his fiancée, Georgette, were a modern couple, quite realistic about the state of marriage these days. They met with the minister of the church to discuss the marriage vows.

"Pastor," said Georgette, "we wonder if we could make a change in the wording of our ceremony."

"Yes, Georgette," replied the pastor, "it is sometimes done. What do you have in mind?"

"Well," said Georgette, looking at Stanley openly, "we'd like to alter the 'until death do us part' section to read, 'Substantial penalty for early withdrawal.'"

☆　☆　☆

Wife: "You're always wishing for something you haven't got."
Man: "What else is there to wish for?"

Just Asking

Why is the third hand on the watch called the second hand?

⭐ ⭐ ⭐

If a word is misspelled in the dictionary, how would we ever know?

⭐ ⭐ ⭐

What happens if you get scared half to death twice?

⭐ ⭐ ⭐

Why do psychics have to ask you for your name?

⭐ ⭐ ⭐

Why do tugboats push their barges?

Why do "slow down" and "slow up" mean the same thing?

☆ ☆ ☆

Why do we say something is out of whack? What is a whack?

☆ ☆ ☆

Why do "fat chance" and "slim chance" mean the same thing?

☆ ☆ ☆

If Barbie is so popular, why do you have to buy her friends?

☆ ☆ ☆

Why are they called "stands" when they are made for sitting?

☆ ☆ ☆

Why is it called "after dark" when it is really "after light"?

☆ ☆ ☆

Why are "wise man" and "wise guy" opposites?

Why do "overlook" and "oversee" mean opposite things?

☆　☆　☆

Why is phonics not spelled the way it sounds?

☆　☆　☆

How can you lose your life's savings on something called securities?

☆　☆　☆

Why do you press harder on the buttons of a remote control when you know the batteries are dead?

☆　☆　☆

Why do we wash bath towels? Aren't we clean when we use them?

☆　☆　☆

Why is the time of day with the slowest traffic called rush hour?

☆　☆　☆

If procrastinators had a club, would they ever have a meeting?

Why is there always one in every crowd?

☆ ☆ ☆

If work is so terrific, why do they have to pay you to do it?

☆ ☆ ☆

Have you ever noticed that just one letter makes all the difference between here and there?

☆ ☆ ☆

If the #2 pencil is the most popular, why is it still #2?

☆ ☆ ☆

Why do we sing "Take Me out to the Ballgame" when we're already there?

☆ ☆ ☆

Isn't it strange that the same people who laugh at gypsy fortune-tellers take economists seriously?

☆ ☆ ☆

If practice makes perfect, and nobody's perfect, why practice?

If all the world's a stage, where does the audience sit?

✩ ✩ ✩

Who decided that Hotpoint would be a good name for a company that sells refrigerators?

✩ ✩ ✩

What if the hokey pokey is really what it's all about?

Knock-Knocks

Knock-knock!
  Who's there?
  Osborn.
  Osborn who?
  Osborn way up in the heels.

☆   ☆   ☆

Knock-knock!
  Who's there?
  Virgil.
  Virgil who?
  Virgil reality seems to be the hot topic of discussion
these days.

Knock-knock!
Who's there?
Amaryllis.
Amaryllis who?
Amaryllis state agent looking for property in your neighborhood.

☆　☆　☆

Knock-knock!
Who's there?
Heaven.
Heaven who?
Heaven you the courtesy to open the door and let me in?

☆　☆　☆

Knock-knock!
Who's there?
Rufus.
Rufus who?
Rufus smokin'. I think your house is on fire.

☆　☆　☆

Knock-knock!
Who's there?
Doughnut.
Doughnut who?
Doughnut keep me waiting out here too long, please.

Knock-knock!
Who's there?
Hair comb.
Hair comb who?
Hair comb the bride!

☆ ☆ ☆

Knock-knock!
Who's there?
Lipset.
Lipset who?
Lipset touch liquor shall never touch mine!

☆ ☆ ☆

Knock-knock!
Who's there?
O.A.
O.A. who?
O.A. down south in Dixie!

☆ ☆ ☆

Knock-knock!
Who's there?
Icon.
Icon who?
Icon operate three programs at one time on my computer.

Knock-knock!
    Who's there?
    Myra.
    Myra who?
    Myra flection is in your window.

Lawyers

A lawyer named Strange died, and his friend asked the tombstone maker to inscribe on his tombstone, "Here lies Strange, an honest man, and a lawyer."

The inscriber insisted that such an inscription would be confusing, for passersby would tend to think that three men were buried under the stone. However he suggested an alternative: He would inscribe, "Here lies a man who was both honest and a lawyer.

"That way," he said, "whenever people walk by the tombstone and read it, they'll be certain to remark: 'That's strange!' "

☆ ☆ ☆

Lawyer: "Here's a draft of the brief I'm about to file in your bankruptcy claim. Better look it over."
Client: "I count thirty pages of solid type. You call this a brief?"

A lawyer was advising a client. "Do you have written documentation that the used car dealer promised to service the car after you bought it?" the attorney asked.

"No, it was a verbal agreement."

"Ach! Verbal agreements aren't worth the paper they're written on."

☆ ☆ ☆

"I love my profession," said the lawyer. "With each new client, it's a challenge, with a brand-new set of facts and a different solution. I never know what to do until I've studied the situation and researched the case law."

"Whereas in my profession," remarked the mortician sadly, "I know exactly what I'm going to do for all my clients before they even come through the door."

☆ ☆ ☆

Two young attorneys fresh out of law school were sharing lunch. "I just got my first case!" one beamed excitedly.

"Oh? Who's the client?"

"Me!"

"You?!? You're representing yourself in your first case?"

"Yeah. I'm being sued."

"By whom?"

"By my dad."

"Your own father is suing you? What for?"

"For the $55,000 he spent sending me to law school."

A newly hired young lawyer was determined to make a big impression at the law firm. His opportunity came soon after he settled into his new office, when the secretary called him on the intercom to let him know a man was there to see him. The young hotshot immediately picked up the phone, and when the prospective client entered his office, the lawyer was talking as though some big deal were cooking. He spoke of a million dollar contract, of some cartel, about a prestigious law firm in another city, and on and on.

Finally, convinced that the man who was waiting must surely be impressed, he hung up the phone and asked him what he could do for him. The man replied, "I'm here to hook up your new phone."

☆　☆　☆

A man was describing to his lawyer the various damages caused by a neighbor's careless landscaping: shattered fence, poisoned shrubbery, drainage problems resulting from soil erosion, etc.

"So you want me to sue for damages?" the lawyer asked.

"No, I don't want you to damage him. I want you to sue him for repairs."

A man called his lawyer and asked, "How much would you charge me to answer three questions?"

The lawyer answered, "Four hundred dollars."

The man said, "That's a lot of money, isn't it?"

The lawyer replied, "I guess so. What is your third question?"

☆ ☆ ☆

Clothes don't necessarily make the man, but a good suit makes a lawyer.

☆ ☆ ☆

A lawyer was cross-examining an elderly witness in a robbery case. He thought he'd capitalize on the probability that her eyesight left something to be desired.

"Mrs. Wilson, would you please tell us your age?"

"I'm seventy-eight years old," she said proudly.

"And have you ever worn eyeglasses?"

"I carry a pair in my purse, but I hardly ever need them."

"Is that so? Now, Mrs. Wilson, how far away from the scene of the crime were you standing?"

"I was down the street a little ways. They tell me it was sixty or seventy yards."

"Are you absolutely certain you can see things clearly at that distance?"

"I suppose so. We're 240,000 miles from the moon, and I can see that just fine on clear nights."

There was a leak in the bathroom, so the lawyer's secretary called the plumber, who came and fixed it in a matter of minutes. The bill, however, was so substantial that the lawyer called to complain.

"You were here for no more than ten minutes. I don't charge that much for an hour."

"I know," responded the plumber sympathetically. "I didn't either when I was a lawyer."

☆ ☆ ☆

Two men, Ed and Bob, set out to cross the Atlantic Ocean in a hot air balloon. After a day and a half aloft, Ed said, "Bob, we ought to drop some altitude so we can see where we are." Bob let some of the air out of the balloon, and the craft descended below the cloud cover. Ed said, "I still can't tell where we are. Let's ask that guy down on the ground."

So Ed yelled to the man, "Hey, can you tell us where we are?"

The man on the ground yells back to the Ed and Bob, "You're in a balloon, 100 feet up in the air."

Bob turned to Ed and said, "I'm guessing that man's a lawyer."

Ed asked, "Why do you think that?"

"Because," Bob replied, "the advice he gave us is one hundred percent accurate, and totally useless."

During a trial, a small town prosecuting attorney called his first witness—a grandmotherly, elderly woman—to the stand. He approached her and asked, "Mrs. Jones, do you know me?"

She responded, "Why, yes, I do know you, Mr. Williams. I've known you since you were a young boy. And frankly, you've been a huge disappointment to me. You lie, you cheat, you manipulate people, and talk about them behind their backs. You think you're a rising big shot when you haven't the brains to realize you'll never amount to anything more than a small-time paper pusher. Oh, yes, I know you."

The lawyer was taken aback. Not knowing what else to do, he pointed across the room and asked, "Mrs. Williams, do you know the defense attorney?"

She again replied, "Why, yes I do. I've known Mr. Bradley since he was a youngster, too. I used to baby-sit him for his parents. And he, too, has been a real disappointment to me. He's lazy and bigoted, and has a drinking problem. The man can't build a normal relationship with anyone, and his law practice is one of the shoddiest in the entire state. Oh, yes, I know him."

At this point, the judge rapped the courtroom to silence and called both counselors to the bench. In a menacing whisper he said to them, "If either of you asks her if she knows me, you'll be in jail for contempt within five minutes!"

The antipathy between a doctor and a lawyer was brought out in the courtroom when the lawyer questioned the doctor:

"Doctor, how many autopsies have you performed on dead people?"

"All my autopsies are performed on dead people."

"In the case of Mr. Dennington, do you recall the time that you examined the body?"

"The autopsy started around 8:30 P.M."

"And Mr. Dennington was dead at that time?"

"No, he was sitting on the table wondering why I was doing an autopsy."

"Doctor, before you performed the autopsy, did you check the pulse?"

"No."

"Did you check the blood pressure?"

"No."

"Did you check for breathing?"

"No."

"So then it was possible that the patient was alive when you began the autopsy?"

"No."

"How can you be sure, Doctor?"

"Because his brain was sitting on my desk in a jar."

"But could the patient have been alive nevertheless?"

"It is possible that he could have been alive and is practicing law somewhere."

Appearing for a conference with a prospective attorney, the client told the details of his case. The attorney mulled it over for a moment and said, "I think we have a pretty strong case."

"I guess I'd better not sue," the client replied. "I told you the other guy's side of the story."

☆　☆　☆

"I need a criminal lawyer," a stranger announced in a small town barber shop. "Know where I might find one around here?"

"Well, Lawyer Blake and Lawyer Black are obvious choices. There are a couple others we suspect, if Blake and Black are both too busy to take your case."

Little Johnny

A new teacher was trying to make use of her psychology courses. She started class by saying, "Everyone who thinks you're stupid, stand up!"

After a few seconds, Little Johnny stood up. The teacher said, "Do you really think you're stupid, Little Johnny?"

"No, ma'am, but I hate to see you standing there all by yourself!"

☆ ☆ ☆

At Sunday school, the teacher was telling the children about how God created everything, including human beings. Little Johnny seemed especially intent when she told him how Eve was created out of one of Adam's ribs.

Later in the week, his mother noticed him lying down as though he were ill, and said, "Johnny, what's the matter?"

Little Johnny responded, "I have a pain in my side. I think I'm going to have a wife."

Little Johnny watched with fascination as his mother smoothed cold cream onto her face. "Why do you do that, Mommy?" he asked.

"To make myself beautiful," his mother replied. She then began removing the cream with a tissue.

"What's the matter?" asked Little Johnny. "Giving up?"

☆ ☆ ☆

The math teacher saw that Little Johnny was paying attention in class. She called on him and said, "Johnny! What are 2 and 4 and 28 and 44?"

Little Johnny quickly replied, "NBC, CBS, ESPN, and the Cartoon Network!"

☆ ☆ ☆

Unhappy at the state of Little Johnny's room, his mother came up with a new rule. Each time she had to pick something up off the floor of his room, Johnny would have to pay her a dime. At the end of the week, she added up the chores and demanded ninety cents. Johnny paid her and said, "Thanks, Ma. Keep up the good work!"

☆ ☆ ☆

While teaching grammar to the class one day, Little Johnny's English teacher pointed to him and said, "Give me two personal pronouns."

"Who, me?" Johnny replied.

Little Johnny was in the garden filling in a hole when his neighbor peered over the fence.

Interested in what the youngster was up to, the neighbor politely asked, "What are you up to there, Johnny?"

"My goldfish died," replied Johnny tearfully, without looking up, "and I've just buried him."

The neighbor was concerned. "That's an awfully big hole for a goldfish, isn't it?"

Johnny patted down the last heap of earth then replied, "That's because he's inside your nasty cat."

☆　☆　☆

Little Johnny used to hang out at the local corner market, and the other boys would constantly tease him. They told him he was two bricks shy of a load, or two pickles short of a barrel. To prove it, they would offer Johnny his choice between a nickel and a dime. Little Johnny would always take the nickel, because it was bigger.

One day after Johnny again chose the nickel, the store owner took him aside and said "Johnny, those boys are making fun of you. Don't you know that a dime is worth more than a nickel?"

Johnny looked up at the store owner and a big grin appeared on his face. He said, "Of course I know that a dime is worth more than a nickel, but if I took the dime, they'd quit asking me to choose, and so far I've saved $20!"

Logic

A young man sitting in a bus depot turned to a middle-aged man nearby and asked him for the time. The middle-aged man said, "I'm not going to give you the time."

"Why not?"

"I'll tell you why. If I gave you the time, you'd thank me. I'd have to concede that you had manners, so I'd probably start talking to you. We'd keep talking on the bus, and by the time we got to Philadelphia we'd be more than mere acquaintances. I might even ask you to come to my house for dinner. You'd meet my lovely daughter and you'd want to start taking her out. After a while, you'd fall in love and you'd propose and she'd say yes. So I won't tell you the time, because I don't want a son-in-law who doesn't even own a watch!"

☆   ☆   ☆

A man told his pastor, "I love to sin. God loves to forgive sin. This world is admirably arranged."

Two commercial bankers were having lunch. One was a twenty-year veteran of the finance industry, the other a novice just out of business school. The younger was picking the other's brain for advice.

"Mr. Morton, what usually happens when a person with a lot of money but no experience goes into partnership with a person who has no money but lots of experience?"

"Either the venture will fail altogether," advised the senior, "or the partner with the experience will end up with all the money."

☆ ☆ ☆

A Swiss man pulled up to a stop and asked directions from two Americans who were standing there.

"Entschulding, können Sie Deutsch sprechen?"

The two Americans just stared at him.

"Excuse-moi, parlez vous francais?" Nothing.

The disgusted man drove off.

"Y'know, maybe we should learn a foreign language."

"Why? That guy knew two languages, and it didn't do him any good."

☆ ☆ ☆

A retired volunteer was presented with an annual award at a community service banquet.

"I really don't deserve this," the honoree told the audience, "but then again, I really don't deserve arthritis, either."

Three university professors—an architectural engineer, a biologist and a philosopher—always shared their morning break at a little bohemian coffee shop on a quiet corner facing the campus housing units. For several years, they absently noticed the comings and goings at a married students' apartment complex. In one particular apartment, they watched the resident students—a young man and his wife—return to their door together after an early morning class. Like clockwork, the couple returned, books under their arms, at precisely the same time each morning.

Reconvening after the long Christmas break one year, the professors were surprised to see the couple emerge from their apartment carrying an infant.

Reasoned the engineer: "Incorrect dimensions."

Reasoned the biologist: "No, a simple matter of reproduction."

Reasoned the philosopher: "Doesn't matter. What's relevant is that if one human being were now to enter the door, the apartment would be empty."

✩ ✩ ✩

"How many officers do you have on your force?" a visiting relative asked a small-town police chief.

"Counting myself, there are three of us."

"Man, don't tell me this little nowhere of a crossroads needs three police officers!"

"If it weren't for us," responded the chief dryly, "it certainly would."

Three hunters in the north woods entered a little cabin where they found shelter and something to eat. The cabin was ordinary except that the stove was suspended from the rafters by a series of wires. This odd arrangement became the object of discussion, and various theories were advanced.

One man was an engineer and he expounded on thermodynamics and how a suspended stove would affect the heating of the room. Another hunter was a psychologist, and he was sure that the stove was suspended so that the owner could crawl under it in a fetal position and thus experience the warmth and security of his mother's womb. The third hunter was a minister, and he declared that the stove was suspended because of the ancient belief in fire and altar worship. Each was quite convinced he had solved the mystery of the suspended stove.

When the owner came back, they asked him about it. "It's really quite simple," he explained. "I had plenty of wire but not enough stove pipe."

☆ ☆ ☆

"Jill told me you told her I told you she was an airhead, and I told you not to tell her I told you that."

"It's her fault. I told her not to tell you I told her what you said."

"Well, don't let it happen again—and don't tell her I told you she told me."

A very businesslike paper boy knocked on the door of a house. When a woman answered, he demanded, "You haven't paid for your paper all month. Pay up right now or you're off the route and you'll be hearing from our collection agency."

The woman looked around her yard and answered, "I've paid you every week, in much the same way you deliver my newspaper. Look. There's a payment envelope in the bushes to the left, one in the bushes to the right, one up in the gutter of the porch and one in the hole in my living room window."

☆ ☆ ☆

"To what do you attribute living to be ninety years old?" the TV talk show host asked the spry guest.

"Oh, it's a simple ritual I've followed for the last half century."

"Would you mind sharing it with our viewers?"

"Each morning when I wake up, I take three deep breaths, thank the good Lord I'm alive, drink the glass of orange juice my wife has waiting beside the bed and glance at the newspaper."

"That's all?"

"Yep. If my name's not among the obituaries, I proceed to get up."

☆ ☆ ☆

What would life be like if there were no hypothetical situations?

"Daddy," a child asked, "didn't you break your nose when you were a little boy?"

"I'm afraid I did."

"Was it the same nose you have now?"

✩　✩　✩

Two archaeologists were pondering the inscription at the foot of the mummy's case. It read simply: 3 B.C.

"What can that mean?" wondered the first archaeologist.

"Hmm. Could be the license plate of the guy who ran him down."

✩　✩　✩

Reluctant bather: "You're sure there are no sharks along this beach?"

Lifeguard: "Highly unlikely. They don't get along with the alligators."

✩　✩　✩

MacDonald, an old highlander, was nonplused at his first encounter with a Thermos bottle. "If ye put hot coffee in it, it keeps the coffee pipin' hot," delightedly explained his seven-year-old granddaughter. "If ye put in ice water, it keeps the water ice cold."

MacDonald shook his head. "Aye, I believe ye," he said. "But how does it know whether ye want it hot or cold. . . ?"

A teacher was giving a lesson on the circulation of the blood. Trying to make the matter clearer he said, "Now, boys, if I stood on my head, the blood, as you know, would run into it, and I should turn red in the face, correct?"

"Yes, sir," the boys responded in unison.

"Then why is it that while I am standing upright in the ordinary position the blood doesn't run into my feet?"

There was silence for a moment before a little fellow shouted, " 'Cause your feet ain't empty."

☆ ☆ ☆

A woman wrote a check at a department store.

"I'll have to ask you to identify yourself," the clerk said.

The customer took a small mirror from her handbag, looked into it keenly and pronounced, "Yes. That's definitely me."

☆ ☆ ☆

A contented diner standing in line to pay at a buffet restaurant couldn't suppress a deep, joyous burp. Most of the people in hearing distance ignored him, but one man took offense.

"You belched in front of my wife," he challenged. "I think you should apologize."

"Oh, I'm so sorry. Was it her turn?"

City cousin: "At our home we have hot and cold tap
water."
Country cousin: "We do, too. Hot in the summer and
cold in the winter."

☆   ☆   ☆

"Did I ever tell you about my adventures eradicating alligators from the streets of Manhattan?"

"There are no alligators on the streets of
Manhattan."

"Nope. Not anymore."

☆   ☆   ☆

Brett: "Why did you write TGIF on the tops of your
shoes? Do you really need to be reminded it's
Friday?"
Moe: "That doesn't stand for 'Thank Goodness It's
Friday.' It stands for 'Toes Go In First.' "

☆   ☆   ☆

Two friends were discussing the relative merits of car
models.

"I'm waiting for a car that'll last me a lifetime,"
said one.

"I hope to live longer than that," said the other.

Mack paid $650 for his gold watch. It was rustproof, shockproof, magneticproof, fireproof and, of course, waterproof. There was only one thing wrong with it: He lost it.

☆　☆　☆

Pessimist: "I'm a miserable failure. Always have been, always will be."
Optimist: "Maybe you just started at the bottom and felt comfortable there."

☆　☆　☆

"Now remember," the driving instructor said to the aging student, "the overriding objective is for your license to expire before you do."

☆　☆　☆

"Why do you always scratch yourself?"
"I'm the only one who knows where I itch."

☆　☆　☆

Trisha: "Do you believe in smoking?"
Michele: "Well, I've seen it with my own eyes, several times."

Media

News never is really news. It just happens to different people from day to day.

☆ ☆ ☆

Folks throughout the city knew they were in trouble when the new owners of the *Tribune* suavely altered the paper's time-honored motto to read: "ALL THE NEWS THAT'S FIT FOR US."

☆ ☆ ☆

A newspaper ran a blistering editorial in which it stated, "We believe half the members of city council are swindlers."

City hall and its political supporters flooded the editor's phone line for three days. Finally, a retraction was promised. It read: "We now believe half the members of city council are not swindlers."

Social studies teacher: "What did you like best about that miniseries on TV?"
Student: "The fact that it's over."

✩ ✩ ✩

Why did Sylvia buy a small-screen TV?
She wanted to shorten the commercials.

✩ ✩ ✩

Teacher: "Why is television called a 'medium'?"
Student: "Because it's neither rare nor well-done."

✩ ✩ ✩

What's the best thing on TV these days?
The "off" button.

✩ ✩ ✩

A reporter covering a Washington scandal called his paper and said, "I'm having a big problem. My exaggerations can't keep up with the facts!"

✩ ✩ ✩

"What do you think of violence on TV?"
"Well, I guess without it, the newscasters wouldn't have anything interesting to report."

"How is Grace enjoying her retirement?"

"Well, she went back to work after a week."

"Oh, no! Why, she's been looking forward to retirement for years."

"That was before she saw what's on daytime television."

☆　☆　☆

What were the first words spoken after TV was invented?

"This is gonna be just another fad. . . ."

☆　☆　☆

A cub reporter was dispatched to cover an earthquake scene. The devastation was extensive and horrible, with buildings crumbled, folks in shock, sporadic fires, and emergency workers racing hither and yon. Overwhelmed, the reporter waxed theological as she called in her story.

"Even God weeps tonight," she began dictating to her editor, "as He looks down at—"

"Forget the quake!" interrupted the editor. "Interview God. Is our photographer still around?"

☆　☆　☆

Cliff: "Why do you watch all those soap operas on TV?"
Bev: "Because I can't see the actors' faces on the radio."

What do you get when you cross a good mystery with a good comedy?

A play that makes you roll in the aisles laughing. . .
and wondering afterward why you behaved that way.

☆　☆　☆

Warren: "Today's news makes me sick."
Matt: "What paper do you read?"
Warren: *"USA Today."*
Matt: "Try *USA Yesterday.*"

Men and Women

In Ireland, a man was met by a leprechaun. The little creature with magical powers told the man, "I can grant you one wish, what will it be?"

"I would like my IQ doubled," the man said.

"Are you sure about that?"

"Yes, absolutely sure."

"You may not like it," he was warned.

"Well, it is what I want."

So the wee one doubled the man's IQ—by turning him into a woman.

☆　☆　☆

A woman came into the den with her hair top-heavy with curlers and clamps. Her husband looked at her, puzzled.

"What are you staring at?" the woman said. "I just set my hair."

The husband replied, "What time does it go off?"

An English professor wrote the words "a woman without her man is nothing" on the blackboard and directed the students to punctuate it correctly.

The men wrote: "A woman, without her man, is nothing."

The women wrote: "A woman: without her, man is nothing."

☆　☆　☆

"Just remember two things," a man told the groom. "There are two ways to handle a woman, but nobody knows either one of them. Also, never argue with your wife when she's tired. . .or when she's rested."

☆　☆　☆

A husband said to his wife, "Did you tell your sister that what I said was in the strictest confidence?"

The wife said, "No I didn't want her to think it was important enough to repeat!"

☆　☆　☆

A young man walked into a hotel barber shop and asked for the works. As he was being shaved, he tried to make time with the manicurist. He suggested dinner.

The manicurist replied, "That wouldn't be right. I'm married."

The young man laughed. "Ask your husband. He wouldn't mind."

"Ask him yourself. He's shaving you!"

At a church picnic, Luke met Emily, the girl of his dreams. They spent the entire day together. As they walked home down the country road from the park, Luke thought he'd take a chance and kiss Emily. There was one problem: Luke was about five feet tall; Emily was six feet tall. Unable to reach her ruby lips, Luke's heart was breaking until he saw a tree stump ahead. Pulling the heavy stump out of the ground, he pushed it over to Emily, stood on it, and give her a long, passionate kiss. Then they walked on again toward Emily's home.

When finally they arrived at Emily's house, Luke said, "Can I kiss you again?"

"Well, I don't know," Emily said, blushing. "I mean—"

"If I don't have a chance, please tell me," Luke replied. "I'm tired of carrying this here stump!"

✩ ✩ ✩

The shades of night were falling fast
    When for a kiss he asked her.
She must have answered yes, because
    The shades came down much faster!

✩ ✩ ✩

A man brought a dyed skunk fur coat to his wife. She asked, "How can such a pretty coat come from such a foul-smelling animal?"

The husband answered, "I don't expect gratitude, but I do deserve a little respect!"

Billy's father picked him up from school to take him to a dental appointment. Knowing that the acting roles for the school play had been posted that day, he asked Billy if he'd gotten a part.

Billy nodded happily and enthusiastically announced, "I play a man who's been married for twenty years."

"That's great, son," his father replied. "Keep up the good work and before you know it they'll be giving you a speaking part."

☆　☆　☆

A middle-aged bachelor found himself in love with a pretty lady. One night they were driving along and, on an impulse, he turned to her and said, "Will you marry me?"

The woman said, "Yes."

This was followed by a long silence until she asked the man, "Won't you say something more?"

He answered, "Ah, I think I've said too much already."

Middle Age

Middle age is when we can do just as much as ever, but would rather not.

☆ ☆ ☆

You've reached middle age when all you exercise is caution.

☆ ☆ ☆

Middle age is when you are sitting home on Saturday night and the telephone rings and you hope it isn't for you.

☆ ☆ ☆

There are three ways to tell when you've reached middle age. The first is the loss of memory. . .and the other two I forget.

Middle age is when you want to see how long your car will last instead of how fast it will go.

☆　☆　☆

Middle age is when work is a lot less fun and fun is a lot more work.

☆　☆　☆

Middle age is when your clothes no longer fit and it's you that needs the alterations.

☆　☆　☆

You know you have reached middle age when weight lifting consists of just standing up.

☆　☆　☆

Middle age is when you stop criticizing the older generation and start criticizing the younger one.

Money

An older and younger man were the only survivors after a ship was lost during a terrible storm. The younger man bemoaned their fate on the tiny island, but the older man said, "It's okay. We are certain to be found."

"How can you be so certain of that?" the younger man wanted to know.

"I give a lot of money every year to my alma mater and my church. Don't worry. They'll find me."

☆ ☆ ☆

A wealthy old man looked around the table at his sons and daughters and their spouses, who were gathered for a family reunion. "Not a single grandchild," he said with a sigh. "Why I'll give a million dollars to the first couple who presents me with a little one to bounce on my knee. Now let's say grace."

When the old man lifted his eyes again, his wife was the only other person at the table.

Mere wealth can't bring us happiness,
    Mere wealth can't make us glad.
But we'll always take a shot, I guess,
    At being rich and sad!

☆　☆　☆

The church held a raffle to raise money. The next morning someone asked the priest, "Who won the Plymouth?"

"Why, Father Murphy did; wasn't he lucky?"

"And who won the Mercury?" the man asked.

"Why, the Monsignor did; wasn't he lucky?"

"And who won the Cadillac?"

"The Cardinal won the Cadillac; wasn't he lucky?"

Then the priest was asked, "And how many tickets did you buy?"

The priest answered, "I didn't buy any. Wasn't I lucky?"

☆　☆　☆

The newly rich real estate developer splurged on a Rolls Royce Silver Shadow. He couldn't wait to show it off. He asked another businessman if he wanted a ride home.

"Whaddaya think?" he couldn't resist asking his passenger after a mile or two. "Pretty snappy, eh? I'll bet you've never ridden in one of these before."

"Actually I have, but this is my first time in the front seat."

A lady called to tell her pastor that her brother had just won a million dollars in a sweepstakes. "But I have a problem," she went on. "My brother has a bad heart and I'm afraid that if I tell him, he may have a heart attack. I'm calling to see, Reverend, if you would be so kind as to break the news to him." The minister agreed to tell the brother he had become a millionaire.

He made some casual conversation for a bit and then asked, "By the way, did you buy a sweepstakes ticket?"

"Yes, I did," said the man with the bad heart.

"I'm here to let you know you won," continued the pastor. "You won a million dollars." When the man seemed unfazed by this great news, the minister asked, "And what will you be doing with all that money?"

The man told him, "I decided that if I won, I would give half of it to the church." Whereupon the minister had a heart attack.

☆ ☆ ☆

A chronic borrower begged an old acquaintance for one hundred dollars. I'll pay you back as soon as I return from Chicago."

"Exactly what day are you returning?" the man asked.

He shrugged and said, "Who's going?"

☆ ☆ ☆

It's so difficult to save money when your neighbors keep buying things you can't afford.

boy swallowed a coin, which got stuck in his throat. His mother ran out to the street looking for help. A man stopped, took the boy by his shoulders, and hit him with a few strong strokes on his back, and the boy coughed the coin out.

"I don't know how to thank you, sir. Are you a doctor?" the mother asked.

"No, I'm not a doctor," the man replied. "I'm from the IRS."

☆ ☆ ☆

I have a lot of "sweet chariot" stocks. The minute I buy them they swing low!

Music

"Cheryl is a true lover of classical music."

"I've figured that out. The 'William Tell Overture' is her favorite piece of music—and she doesn't know who the Lone Ranger is."

☆ ☆ ☆

Two symphony critics were comparing notes after a concert. "The conductor was fantastic, I thought," said one. "Did you observe how the very first crescendo literally filled the music hall?"

"Yes," said the other. "A substantial number of the audience removed themselves to give it room."

☆ ☆ ☆

What's the difference between bagpipes and a lawn mower?

You can tune a lawn mower.

The pest control man arrived at a home and heard a horrendous barrage of attempted piano music coming through the front screen door. He knocked and waited. The noise didn't abate. He peered inside and could see a teenage lad savagely pounding through a lesson at the keyboard.

The pest control man knocked louder and finally got the woeful student's attention.

"Are your folks at home, son?" he asked.

The boy menacingly banged out a couple of concluding nonchords and glared at the visitor. "Take a wild guess."

☆　☆　☆

Why do bagpipers march when they play?

To get away from the noise.

☆　☆　☆

The story is told of a piano recital by a child prodigy. In the audience a world-renowned pianist was seated next to a famous operatic tenor.

The child made the keys dance so gracefully that every listener in the hall was raised to heavenly heights. . . except the veteran pianist. Perceiving an up-and-coming competitor to his own preeminence, he squirmed visibly in his seat.

"It's dreadfully warm in here," he whispered, pulling at his collar.

"Not for vocalists," replied the tenor.

They laughed when I sat down to play. . .for the piano had no bench.

☆ ☆ ☆

What's the difference between a bagpipe and an onion?
No one cries when you slice a bagpipe.

☆ ☆ ☆

A lady aboard a cruise ship was not impressed by the jazz trio in one of the shipboard restaurants. When her waiter came around, she asked, "Will they play anything I ask?"

"Of course, madam."

"Then tell them to go play shuffleboard."

☆ ☆ ☆

A jazz musician and country-western singer were visiting a small dictatorship, when they ran afoul of the law and were sentenced to death by firing squad. At dawn, they were led to a courtyard where the squad leader asked the country-western singer if he had a final request.

"I'd like to hear six choruses of 'Achy-Breaky Heart,'" the singer replied.

"I think that can be arranged," said the squad leader. Then he turned to the jazz musician. "And your final request?"

"Please," begged the musician, "shoot me first."

McLaramie: "Had a bloody racket at home t'other evenin'. Family above us were stompin' the floor and just ahollerin' til the wee hours o' the marnin'."

McClintock: "Kept ye awake, did it?"

McLaramie: "No, fortunately, I was up already, playin' me bagpipes."

☆ ☆ ☆

When a policeman rang, a scared looking child appeared at the door.

Child: "What do you want?"

Policeman: "We had a telephone call that a fellow named Beethoven was being murdered in this house."

☆ ☆ ☆

The band was nervous. So was the new music teacher. Before their first concert, he told the kids that if they weren't sure of their part, just pretend to play.

When the big moment arrived, the parents waited expectantly. The teacher brought down the baton with a mighty flourish, and lo, the band gave forth with a resounding silence.

☆ ☆ ☆

Music teacher: "In the basic choir, there are two male vocal parts. One is the tenor. What is the other?"

Student: "Er—niner?"

A great pianist once was asked by a young prodigy for his advice on how to become the greatest pianist in history.

"My best advice," said the older man, "is to begin practicing while you are very young, learn all you can from your elders, and by the time you've reached the end of your life, you will have attained your goal."

"But you were great before the age of twenty," the youngster protested.

"Perhaps," acknowledged his mentor. "But I never had to ask anyone's advice."

☆ ☆ ☆

Woman to Organist: "Your preludes are so loud, I can't hear what my friends are saying."

☆ ☆ ☆

A couple was standing in the ticket line at the concert hall when the husband remarked, "I wish we'd brought along our piano bench."

"What in the world for?"

"Because the tickets are inside the seat."

☆ ☆ ☆

A community chorus conductor came home from the first rehearsal in a sour temper.

"Not much talent?" asked her husband.

"In a way, they have talent, I suppose," she replied. "They sing like the Mormon Tabernacle rugby team."

What's the best way to tune a tuba?
With a hacksaw.

☆ ☆ ☆

The symphony musicians had little confidence in the person brought in to be their new conductor. Their fears were realized at the very first rehearsal. The conductor's wand was unsteady and he had them playing at atrocious tempos and volumes. Soon, the sound became more dissonant than that of a first-year elementary school band.

The cymbalist had heard enough. During a delicate, soft passage, he suddenly clashed his instruments together with all the force and fury he could muster.

The music stopped. The conductor, highly agitated, looked angrily around the orchestra, demanding, "Who did that? Who did that?"

☆ ☆ ☆

What has eight hands and plays "Rocky Top"?
A bluegrass band.

☆ ☆ ☆

Jenny: "So you're a professional rock musician? That's exciting!"
Wally: "Yeah, I guess I've played the hits in half the nightclubs in New York City."
Jenny: "Why aren't you still playing music?"
Wally: "My quarters ran out."

An operatic tenor was consulting his doctor in desperation. "You've got to do something for this head cold," he demanded.

"I can give you medicine to relieve the symptoms," the doctor explained, "but you'll still have the cold. It simply has to run its course. You know that."

"But it won't do, this week. Whenever I get a head cold, in a few days it goes to my throat, then to my chest—and I have my most important performance of the year coming up Friday night! I insist that you do something."

"Well, perhaps we can tie your neck in a knot until Friday. That might delay the cold's progress."

✧ ✧ ✧

An inexperienced cello instructor began his first class nervously. He squawked a few melodies to demonstrate the sound of the instrument, then gave a brief lecture about the instrument.

"My own cello," he mentioned proudly, "is an exceptional instrument—quite expensive. Yours are only beginners' models, of course. But in the hands of a practiced musician, any cello will provide many years of rich, sonorous, exquisite music."

One student nudged another and said sadly, "I'm afraid some other practiced musician used up all the rich, sonorous, exquisite music his cello had, a long time ago."

"I've swallowed my harmonica!" shrieked Jones.

"Good thing you don't play banjo," drawled the doctor.

☆　☆　☆

Q: What happens when you play country music backwards?

A: Your dog comes back, you get your truck back, your momma gets out of jail. . . .

Neighbors

"I think the Smiths are suffering from age-related strife," a woman said of her neighbors.

"What do you mean?" asked her husband.

"He won't act his age, and she won't admit hers."

☆ ☆ ☆

A secret agent was directed to a posh condominium complex to contact an anonymous source. "Williams is the name," he was told by his superior. "Hand him this envelope."

Arriving at the complex, he was confused to find four different Williamses occupying adjacent quarters. He decided to try the second condo. When a gentleman answered his knock, the agent spoke the pass code: "The grape arbor is down."

Looking him over, the man shook his head. "I'm Williams the accountant. You might try Williams the spy. Two doors down."

The prospective buyer of a home in an exclusive subdivision had to appear before the neighborhood association's screening committee.

"Do you have small children?" was the first question.

"No."

"Outdoor pets?"

"No."

"Do you play any musical instrument at home?"

"No."

"Do you often host personal or business guests who might arrive in more than two vehicles at one time?"

"No." And by now, the prospect had decided the restrictions weren't for him. He held up his hand, rose from his chair and told the panel, "We may as well call off the deal right now. You need to be aware I sneeze on the average of two or three times a week."

☆ ☆ ☆

"I see the Andersons have returned our grill," said the wife happily, glancing out the window. "They've had it for the last six months, and I was afraid now that they're moving, they'd take it with them by mistake."

"You mean that was our grill?" screamed her husband, entering the back door. "I just paid $25 for it at their yard sale!"

☆ ☆ ☆

The best neighbors are the ones who make their loudest noises at the same time you're making yours.

Policeman to bystander: "I thought you said you saw a
man jump from the top of the apartment complex."
Bystander: "Yes. It was poor old Larry. I recognized him
from a distance."
Policeman: "We've searched the premises, and we
couldn't find anyone."
Bystander: "Did you check inside? Knowing Larry, he
probably had to stop and ask directions."

☆　☆　☆

"Dad, I think the Browns next door are angry at us."
　"Why is that?"
　"They're probably mad because our dog can retrieve
the newspaper, and theirs can't."
　"How could you possibly know that? We don't even
subscribe to the paper."
　"Yeah, that's probably got something to do with
it, too."

☆　☆　☆

A door-to-door salesman approached a nice home where
two children were playing in the front yard. "Are either
of your parents home?" he called.
　"Yeah, they're both home."
　The salesman rang the bell and waited. He rang
again. Still, no one answered the door.
　"Why won't they come to the door?" he asked the
children.
　"This isn't our house," said one.

Nonsense

A bear went into a shoe store. The clerk was amazed, watching the bear try on oversized loafers and wingtips. The bear found a pair of $50 loafers and gave the clerk a $100 bill.

Figuring the bear didn't understand money and math, the clerk handed back a ten and remarked, "You're the first bear I've ever had for a customer."

"And with your prices, I'm sure I'll be the last."

☆ ☆ ☆

Ron: "Why do matadors wave bright red capes at bulls?"
Rachel: "To make the bulls angry so they'll charge."
Ron: "You mean bulls don't like bright red?"
Rachel: "Oh, bulls don't mind. It's chickens that don't like bright red."
Ron: "So what does that have to do with bullfights?"
Rachel: "A bull really hates being treated like a chicken."

A Martian spacecraft landed just outside a big American city. The crew managed to sneak into town without being noticed until one of the Martians saw a garbage truck round a corner too fast, throwing off a sheet of scrap metal. He automatically waved and yelled, "Hey, lady, you dropped your handkerchief!"

☆ ☆ ☆

A baby hippopotamus was playing hide and seek in the jungle with an ant. The ant, logically, had an easier time concealing himself. Finally, in frustration, the young hippo deliberately stepped on the poor ant.

"Bruce!" shouted the hippo's mother, seeing what had happened. "Why did you kill that ant?"

"I only meant to trip him," Bruce said sheepishly.

☆ ☆ ☆

A woman in Ireland happened to meet an old friend, who was blind, and asked how she was faring.

"Well," the blind woman said, "I've had to give up me skydivin'."

"Skydivin'! I didn't know ye could do that!"

"Oh, yes. And a fine time I was havin'. But it didn't agree with me dog."

☆ ☆ ☆

A horse nosed his way into a convenience store and asked for a pack of cigarettes.

"Are you eighteen?" asked the clerk.

During a break in the action of an international chess match, a group of players gathered in the hotel lobby to trade stories.

As the group members began telling their favorite tales—usually describing how well they performed in previous tournaments—they became louder and louder.

Finally the manager of the hotel walked over to the group and told them that they would have to find another place to talk.

When a group member asked why, the manager responded, "Because no one wants to hear chess nuts boasting by an open foyer."

☆ ☆ ☆

A psychiatrist looked up to see a short, stout man standing in the office doorway, stuffing a peanut butter sandwich into the beak of a parrot atop his head.

"What can I do for you?" the psychiatrist asked.

"Make him lose the sandwich!" hollered the parrot. "I hate peanut butter."

☆ ☆ ☆

Pam: "Did you know 'fat' and 'slim' are really the same thing?"
Sam: "Get outa here. They're the opposite."
Pam: "Then what's the difference between a 'fat chance' and a 'slim chance'?"

Fred: "Wanna hear a couple of great jokes?"
Ted: "Sure."
Fred: "Great joke. Great joke."

✩ ✩ ✩

A rope walked into a restaurant, sat down, and asked the waitress for a cup of coffee.

"We don't serve ropes here," the waitress replied.

So the rope got up, walked out, and crossed the street to another restaurant, but he got the same response. He tried a third restaurant with no luck.

Finally, the rope decided that he would have to disguise himself if he was ever to get some coffee. He ducked into an alley, tied himself into a knot, and roughed up his ends. Then he walked into another restaurant, sat down, and ordered coffee. The waitress eyed him suspiciously, and finally asked, "Hey, pal, are you a rope?"

"Frayed knot," replied the rope.

Old Folks

After his annual checkup, the doctor told the elderly man, "There's no reason why you can't have a completely normal life, as long as you don't try to enjoy it."

☆ ☆ ☆

An elderly, wealthy man was explaining to a friend that he had fallen in love with a much younger woman. "Do you think I should tell her I'm seventy?" he asked his friend. "Or do you think I should tell her I'm sixty?"
His friend advised, "You should tell her you're ninety."

The ninety-year-old woman was out of the room when the minister came to visit her in the nursing home. He began munching on a bowl of peanuts she had on a table.

She came in and apologized for not being there when he came in.

He said, "Oh, that's all right, but I'm sorry I ate all of your peanuts."

"Oh, pastor, don't worry about that," she told him. "I really don't eat peanuts anyway. I just like to suck the chocolate off of them."

✮ ✮ ✮

A ninety-year-old gentleman entered a life insurance office and told the agent he wanted to take out a $300,000 whole-life policy.

"But you're simply too old," the agent said after a moment's consideration. "No insurance company would start a new policy on a ninety-year-old client."

"Sonny boy," the applicant steamed, "are you aware of the mortality demographics within the United States of America?"

"Why, yes, sir. I believe I know the statistics pretty well."

"What percentage of the population dies between the ages of ninety and 120?"

"Er, something less than five percent. . ."

"Then what, exactly, is your problem with my age?"

An elderly man told his pastor about a variety of health problems. His hearing was going as well as his eyesight. He couldn't remember things. He ended by saying, "I don't know why God just doesn't take me."

His pastor tried to reassure him by saying, "God must still have something for you to do."

The old man snapped, "Well, I'm not going to do it."

☆　☆　☆

A big time celebrity was doing a benefit at a senior citizens home. He asked one of them, "Do you know who I am?"

"No, but ask at the front desk—they can tell you."

One Liners

The early bird may get the worm, but the second mouse gets the cheese.

☆ ☆ ☆

Depression is merely anger without enthusiasm.

☆ ☆ ☆

Eagles may soar, but weasels don't get sucked into jet engines.

☆ ☆ ☆

I drive way too fast to worry about my cholesterol.

☆ ☆ ☆

Many people quit looking for work when they find a job.

Success is relative. The more success, the more relatives!

☆ ☆ ☆

Why is crab grass so crabby? It's winning!

☆ ☆ ☆

One of life's mysteries is how a two-pound box of candy can make a person gain five pounds.

☆ ☆ ☆

When everything's coming your way, you're on the wrong side of the freeway.

Only in America?

Only in America. . .can a pizza get to your house faster than an ambulance.

Only in America. . .are there handicap parking spaces in front of a skating rink.

Only in America. . .do people order double cheese burgers, a large fry, and a diet coke.

Only in America. . .do banks leave both doors open and then chain the pens to the counters.

Only in America. . .do we leave cars worth thousands of dollars in the driveway and leave useless things and junk in boxes in the garage.

Only in America. . .do we buy hot dogs in packages of ten and buns in packages of eight.

Only in America. . .do we use answering machines to screen calls and then have call waiting so we won't miss a call from someone we didn't want to talk to in the first place.

Outdoors

Michelle: "Mom, Mom, we just found a snake in the backyard!"

Mom: "Oh, no! Has it bitten anyone?"

Michelle: "Nah. Actually, it's just a baby. It's kinda cute!"

Mom: "Well, you know some snakes never grow very long. How can you be sure it's a baby?"

Michelle: "Because it's carrying its own rattle."

☆ ☆ ☆

Mark: "The scoutmaster says he won't take me along on any more camping trips."

Sharon: "Why not? What did you do?"

Mark: "I think he's angry because I lost the compass when we waded across the creek."

Sharon: "He's mad because a little compass got lost?"

Mark: "Well, it wasn't just the compass that got lost. We all got lost."

Two friends who were camping spotted a big, mean-looking grizzly bear coming toward their camp. One started putting on his running shoes. The other said, "What are you doing that for? You don't think you can outrun a grizzly bear, do you?"

"I don't have to," the other replied. "All I have to do is outrun you."

☆ ☆ ☆

An obscure, lofty peak in Alaska had never been scaled until two American climbers reached the summit after a grueling three-day ordeal. At the end of their strength, they lay in the thin air and rested for several hours. Then, ready to begin the descent, one said, "Okay, let's plant the American flag and head back down."

The partner turned with a frown. "I thought you brought the flag."

☆ ☆ ☆

A hiker followed a trail out of the woods and found himself at a crossroads store. Disoriented, he approached a woman who stood outside.

"Can you tell me how far Hooterville is?" he asked.

"I'm afraid not."

"Well, which of these roads goes north?"

"I'm not sure."

The hiker was exasperated. "Don't you know anything? What village is this?"

"I don't know that, either. I'm just passing through."

Two retired friends were lounging at poolside when one commented, "I feel like hiking three miles in the mountains this weekend."

"Well, just stay in bed," the friend said. "The feeling will pass."

☆ ☆ ☆

A couple of American tourists were on their own in South America and got lost. Stopping a local pedestrian, one tourist asked, "Can you tell us the general direction of the Andes Mountains?"

"Up," replied the local.

☆ ☆ ☆

The story is told of Daniel Webster who, after a day of hunting, found himself far from home at nightfall. After groping through the darkness awhile, he came upon a farmhouse and knocked repeatedly at the door. It was several minutes before the farmer opened an upstairs window and held a lantern out to see who was down there.

"What do you want?" the farmer asked gruffly.

"I wish to spend the night here," Webster implored.

"Good. Spend the night there." The lantern went out and the window closed.

Parents and Children

A father was reading Bible stories to his young son. He read, "The man named Lot was warned to take his wife and flee out of the city, but his wife looked back and was turned to salt."

His son asked, "What happened to the flea?"

☆ ☆ ☆

When little Molly Brown told people her name, they would often say, "Oh, you must be Reverend Brown's daughter."

She told her mother that she just wanted to be herself.

Her mother told her, "The next time that happens, just stand right up and say, 'I am Molly Brown.'"

A few days later, some people met her, and when they heard her name, they said, "Why, Reverend Brown must be your father."

The little girl looked them right in the eye and said, "Oh, no! That's not what my mother says."

"Dad, will you help me with my homework?"

"I'm sorry, son. It wouldn't be right."

"Well, at least you could try."

☆ ☆ ☆

A man observed a woman in the grocery store with a three-year-old girl in her basket. As they passed the cookie section, the child asked for cookies and her mother told her no. The little girl immediately began to whine and fuss, and the mother said quietly, "Now Ellen, we just have half of the aisles left to go through; don't be upset. It won't be long."

The man passed the mother again in the candy aisle. Of course, the little girl began to shout for candy. When she was told she couldn't have any, she began to cry. The mother said, "There, there, Ellen, don't cry. Only two more aisles to go, and then we'll be checking out."

The man again happened to be behind the pair at the checkout, where the little girl began to clamor for gum and burst into a terrible tantrum upon discovering there would be no gum purchased today. The mother patiently said, "Ellen, we'll be through this checkout stand in five minutes, and then you can go home and have a nice nap."

The man followed them out to the parking lot and stopped the woman to compliment her. "I couldn't help noticing how patient you were with little Ellen."

The mother looked at him with bewilderment. "I'm Ellen. My little girl's name is Tammy."

Anyone who thinks you can't buy happiness has never sent the kids away to summer camp.

☆ ☆ ☆

For parents, a Little League baseball game is a nervous breakdown divided into innings.

☆ ☆ ☆

Children need a pat on the back, provided it is applied soon enough, hard enough, and low enough.

☆ ☆ ☆

A father and his daughter were watching television while the mother and son did the dishes. There was a crash from the kitchen.

"Oops, Mom broke a dish," the daughter said.

"How do you know it was Mom?" her father asked.

"Because she's not saying anything."

☆ ☆ ☆

A mother had just put her young son to bed for the umpteenth time and her patience was wearing thin. "If I hear you say 'Mother' one more time, I'm going to come up there and spank you," she warned him sternly.

For a while it was quiet, and then she heard a small voice call from the top of the stairs, "Mrs. Green? Can I have a drink of water?"

Kids will never understand why parents make them go to bed when they're wide awake and make them get up when they're sleepy!

☆　☆　☆

A little boy was asked, "Why are you walking around and around the block?"

"I'm running away," he answered. "But how can you run away if you stay on the same block?"

He answered, "That's because I'm not allowed to cross the street."

☆　☆　☆

A rabbi, priest, and minister were discussing the theological question: "When does life begin?" The priest said he believed it was at the moment of conception. The minister said he believed it was at the moment of birth. The rabbi nodded and told the others that he understood their points of view. "But," he added, "after considerable thought and experience, I've come to the conclusion that life begins when the children leave home."

☆　☆　☆

A mother and her young son returned from the grocery store and began putting away the groceries. The boy opened the box of animal crackers and spread them all over the table. "What are you doing?" his mother asked.

"The box says not to eat them if the seal is broken," the boy explained. "I'm looking for the seal."

A young boy went with his dad to see a litter of kittens.

Upon returning home, he breathlessly informed his mother, "There were two boy kittens and two girl kittens."

"How did you know?" his mother asked.

"Daddy picked them up and looked underneath," the boy replied. "I think it's written on the bottom."

☆ ☆ ☆

A mother was preparing pancakes for her sons, Kevin, 5, and Ryan, 3. The boys began to argue over who would get the first pancake. Their mother saw the opportunity for a moral lesson. "If Jesus were sitting here, He would say, 'Let my brother have the first pancake. I can wait.'"

Kevin turned to his younger brother and said, "Ryan, you be Jesus!"

☆ ☆ ☆

A three-year-old boy put his shoes on by himself. His mother noticed that the left shoe was on the right foot. She said, "Son, your shoes are on the wrong feet."

He looked up at her with a raised brow and said, "Don't kid me, Mom. I KNOW they're my feet."

☆ ☆ ☆

"If Dad should die," the small boy asked his mother, "do you think there's another man in the world just like him?"

"Probably," she replied, "and it would be just my luck to get him."

A son with a brand new Master's of Business Administration degree came home to visit his parents, who owned a little "mom and pop" store. The young expert in business criticized his father for his inept business practices. "You keep your accounts receivable on a spindle, your accounts payable in a cigar box, and your cash in a drawer," he complained. "How do you know your profit?" he asked.

"Son," his father gently explained, "it's like this. When I got off the boat, I owned nothing but the pants I had on. Now we have a home, a car, a business—all paid for. Your sister is an art teacher, your brother is a doctor, and you have an MBA. Add that all up and subtract the pants and there's your profit."

☆ ☆ ☆

While a little boy was gone to school one day, his cat got run over by a truck.

His mother was very concerned about how he would take the news. Upon his arrival home, she explained the tragedy and tried to console the boy by saying, "But don't worry, Bootsie is in heaven with God now."

To which the boy replied, "What's God gonna do with a dead cat?"

☆ ☆ ☆

A boy came home with a bad report card. As he handed it to his father, he asked, "What do you think's wrong, Dad, my heredity or my environment?"

The mother of a small girl, concerned about her child's selfish behavior, was giving her a lecture about how she had been put in this world to help others.

Her daughter seemed much impressed and sat silently, thinking and scratching her head. At last she looked up and said, "Mommy?"

"Yes, dear?" replied her mother.

"What I want to know is, what are the others here for?"

☆ ☆ ☆

A small girl's father asked her what she wanted for Christmas. "A baby brother," she said.

Later that year, her mother came home from the hospital with a baby boy. The little girl was delighted.

"And what would you like this year for Christmas?" her father asked.

She said, "If it isn't too uncomfortable for mother, I would like a pony."

☆ ☆ ☆

A father was at the beach with his children when his four-year-old son ran up to him, grabbed his hand, and led him to the water's edge, where a sea gull lay dead in the sand. "Daddy, what happened to him?" the son asked.

"He died and went to heaven," the dad replied.

The boy thought for a moment and then said, "Did God throw him back down?"

A little boy got lost and found himself in the women's locker room. When he was spotted, the room burst into shrieks with ladies grabbing towels and running for cover. The little boy watched in amazement and then asked, "What's the matter—haven't you ever seen a little boy before?"

☆ ☆ ☆

A four-year-old girl was learning to say the Lord's Prayer. She was reciting it all by herself without help from her mother. She said, "And lead us not into temptation, but deliver us some E-mail."

☆ ☆ ☆

A young minister preached a sermon he entitled "Rules for Raising Children." Then he got some kids of his own and changed the sermon title to "Suggestions for Raising Children." When his kids got to be teenagers he stopped preaching on the subject altogether.

☆ ☆ ☆

"Wasn't it good of the shepherds to put on clean clothes when they went to see baby Jesus?" the little boy stated.

His mother asked, "How do you know they did that?"

Johnny replied, "In Sunday school we sang 'While Shepherds Washed Their Socks by Night.'"

"Dear Mom and Dad," a daughter wrote from college. "Since I left for college I've not written like I promised to do. I will bring you up to date now, but before you read this, please sit down. I am getting along pretty well now. The skull fracture and concussion I got when I jumped out of the dormitory when it caught fire are pretty well healed. I was in the hospital only two weeks and I can see almost normally again. I only get sick headaches once a day now. Fortunately, the attendant at a gas station near the dorm saw the fire and called the fire department and the ambulance. He also visited me in the hospital and was kind enough to invite me to share his apartment since I had no place to live after the dorm burned down.

"He is really a fine boy. We hope to get married before my pregnancy begins to show, if the blood test comes out all right. I know you will welcome him into our family with open arms even though he is of a different race and religion. I know how much you look forward to being grandparents and will welcome the baby and give it the same love and devotion you gave me when I was a child."

Then she added as a postscript:

"The truth is, there was no dormitory fire. I did not have a concussion or a skull fracture. I'm not engaged. I'm not sharing an apartment with anyone, and I'm not expecting a baby. However, I am getting a D in history and an F in science and I wanted you to see those marks in their proper perspective."

"I hear your son is a Ramblin' Wreck from Georgia Tech," a man said to his friend.

"No," came the reply, "he flunked out there and now he's a total loss at Holy Cross."

Perspective

One nice thing about egotists: They don't talk about other people.

☆ ☆ ☆

Procrastination is the art of keeping up with yesterday.

☆ ☆ ☆

Women like silent men; they appear to be listening.

☆ ☆ ☆

Give a man a fish and he will eat for a day. Teach him how to fish and he will sit in a boat all day.

☆ ☆ ☆

Age is a very high price to pay for maturity.

"Dad, is it true that people judge you by the company you keep?"

"I'm afraid so, son."

"Well, then, if two guys hang out together, and one's good and the other's bad, does that mean people think the good guy is bad and the bad guy is good?"

☆　☆　☆

A couple and their small child made their way onto a crowded bus. There were no seats vacant, so they all had to stand in the aisle as the bus bounced along the streets.

The child was licking an ice cream cone, trying unsuccessfully to stay ahead of the melting vanilla mess. Sadly, the woman seated nearest the youngster wore an expensive fur coat. More than once, the ice cream brushed against the brownish-black fur.

When the woman finally noticed what was happening, she shrieked, "My coat! It has dreadful, sticky ice cream in it!"

Examining the ice cream cone, the child shrieked, "My ice cream! It's got hair in it!"

☆　☆　☆

"Your boyfriend is cute. I love that blond hair and those blue eyes."

"Yeah, he's got a twin, too."

"Really! Can you tell them apart easily?"

"Well, if you look close, you'll notice his sister's a little bit shorter."

Marcie has a master's degree in physical science. Each day, she asks, "Why does this work?"

Kevin has a master's degree in mechanical engineering. Each day, he asks, "How does this work?"

Brit has a master's degree in economics. Each day, she asks, "How much does it cost to manufacture this?"

Chuck has a master's degree in chemistry. Each day, he asks, "Could this be hazardous to the environment?"

Alvin has a master's degree in liberal arts. Each day, he asks, "Would you like fries with your cheeseburger?"

✮ ✮ ✮

Three crews were competing for a contract with a telephone company. In order to select the most qualified, the phone company instructed each crew to go out and see how many poles they could put up in one day.

At the end of the day, one crew reported thirty-five poles. The second reported thirty-two poles. The third crew boasted that they had installed five poles.

"Why are you so proud of yourselves?" the foreman asked the third crew. "These other guys did thirty-five and thirty-two respectively."

"Yeah," the third crewmen said, "but did you see how much of the poles they left sticking out of the ground?"

✮ ✮ ✮

A little boy asked one of his sister's suitors, "How come you show up every night to see my sister when you have one of your own?"

The Pessimist: Looks for a coffin whenever he smells flowers.

Believes life is a car wash and he's riding a bike.

Looks at the land of milk and honey and sees nothing but calories and cholesterol.

Stays up on New Year's Eve to make sure the old year leaves.

Looks both ways before crossing a one-way street.

☆ ☆ ☆

A shoe manufacturer sent two salesmen to a remote country. Not long after, he received a telegram from each. One wrote: "Get me out of here—no one wears shoes." The other wrote: "Send me more inventory—everyone needs shoes."

☆ ☆ ☆

A little boy kept bragging to his father about what a great hitter he was. Finally the father said, "All right, son, show me."

The boy grabbed his bat and ball, and they went out to the back yard.

The boy tossed the ball up, swung with all his might, and missed. "Strike one," he said. Again the ball went up without the bat making contact. "Strike two." The boy tossed it a third time. "Strike three."

Without missing a beat, the boy put down his bat, picked up his glove and announced, "Boy, am I a great pitcher."

A man was greeted by his wife, who always had a cheerful word for him when he came home from work. "Guess what?" she said. "Of our five children, four of them did not break an arm today."

☆ ☆ ☆

Mary: "I hear Skip was a real hero when the office building caught fire. They say he led the whole staff safely outside."

Irvin: "Something like that. Actually, what I heard was that Skip was the first one out the door."

☆ ☆ ☆

Bob walked into the living room where his father was reading. "Pop," he said enthusiastically, "I've got great news for you."

His father smiled and asked, "What is that?"

"Remember you promised me five bucks if I raised my grades?" His father nodded.

"Well," Bob said, "I'm sparing you that expense."

☆ ☆ ☆

The teacher brought Mike to the principal's office for punishment. "This is the fourth time this week that you've been in here to be paddled," the principal said. "What do you have to say for yourself?"

"I'm glad today is Friday."

Politicians

Bulldozer: Someone who sleeps through a political speech.

☆ ☆ ☆

After he lost the election, the candidate said, "I feel like the missionary who went out to convert the cannibals. They listened with the greatest of interest to everything he had to say. Then they ate him."

☆ ☆ ☆

Late one night, a mugger wearing a ski mask jumped into the path of a well-dressed man and stuck a gun in his ribs. "Give me your money," he demanded.

Indignant, the affluent man replied, "You can't do this, I'm a United States Congressman!"

"In that case," replied the mugger, "give me MY money."

"I see old Senator Jones isn't quite as big a windbag as he used to be," said Elliott after a political rally.

"You think he's mellower these days?"

"Oh, no, but he has lost a little weight."

☆   ☆   ☆

"How does it feel to get so much criticism from the press?" a politician was asked.

He answered, "I feel like the javelin competitor who won the toss of the coin and elected to receive."

☆   ☆   ☆

Did you hear about the latest government study on aging? It cost $240 million and provided compelling evidence that the average American is growing older.

☆   ☆   ☆

The politician concluded a boisterous but shallow speech filled with impossible promises sure to appeal to the particular audience. Mingling with the crowd afterward, he happened on a wise, respected old city father. Hoping for a compliment within hearing of some of the audience, he asked the old man what he thought of the speech.

"Well," the gentleman said thoughtfully, "I think for those who want to hear about those kinds of things, those were exactly the kinds of statements they wanted to hear."

A candidate and his wife fell into the hotel bed at the end of a long day on the campaign trail.

"I'm exhausted," groaned the wife.

"I think I have more right to be exhausted than you do," complained the candidate. "I delivered six speeches in six towns today."

"And I had to listen to the same message six times," his wife replied.

☆ ☆ ☆

A group of state-level politicians, taking a bus tour of their territory, did not return to the capital as expected. Since nobody had heard from the group since it left that morning, a search party was organized.

The investigators followed the politicians' itinerary, driving from one town to the next to determine where the group might be. Finally, the searchers found the politicians' bus, lying on its side along the road. But the occupants were nowhere to be found.

The searchers quickly ran to a nearby farmhouse to see if the politicians were inside. An old farmer answered their knock, and told the investigators that, yes, he had seen the bus crash, but, no, the politicians were not inside his home.

"Where are they?" the lead investigator asked.

"I buried 'em," the farmer replied.

"You buried them?" the investigator asked incredulously. "Surely, they weren't all dead?"

"Well, they kept saying they weren't dead," the farmer admitted. "But you know how those politicians lie!"

Governor Christian Herter of Massachusetts stopped for a plate of food at a picnic while campaigning. When the woman who was serving the food put a piece of barbecued chicken on his plate, Herter said, "I'm tired and hungry. I would like two pieces." When she informed him that a portion was one piece per person, he snapped, "Do you know who I am? I am the governor."

Without batting an eye, the woman replied, "Do you know who I am? I'm the lady in charge of chicken." He left with one piece of chicken on his plate.

☆ ☆ ☆

Two rival candidates for a local government seat happened to meet at a taxi stand. Smith was a wealthy veteran of city hall politics, Brown a middle-income political novice.

"I hate to tell you this, son," said Smith, condescending to offer a bit of frank advice, "but you need money if you ever want to run a successful campaign in this city. Lots of money." He took a wad of bills from a coat pocket. "See this? I always carry plenty of cash and spread it around liberally. For example, when my cabby drops me off, I'll give him a wink, a smile and a $5 bill, and let him know I'm counting on his vote."

Young Brown got to thinking about the tactic and came up with a shoestring-budget variation. When his cab driver dropped him off, he quickly stepped out the door without leaving any tip at all. "Be sure to vote for Smith in the city council race next Tuesday," he called over his shoulder.

One candidate at a political rally held the podium a full forty minutes with what had to be the most meaningless, boring speech in the county's history. Finally, he concluded and asked if anyone in the audience had a question.

"I do," piped up a voice. "Who's your opponent?"

Potpourri

A Greek tailor in Chicago had a lighthearted routine for customers who brought in torn dress coats or pants for repair. "Euripides?" he would ask.

To which knowing regulars would respond, "That's right. Eumenides?"

✧ ✧ ✧

A bunch of chickens were in the yard when a football flew over the fence and landed in their midst. A rooster waddled over, studied it, then said, "Not to be critical, ladies, but look at the work they're turning out next door."

A knight and his men returned to the castle after a long hard day of fighting.

"How are we faring?" asked the king.

"Sire," replied the knight, "I have been robbing and pillaging on your behalf all day, burning the towns of your enemies to the west."

"What?!" shouted the king. "I don't have any enemies to the west!"

"Oh!" exclaimed the embarrassed knight. "Well, you do now. . . ."

☆ ☆ ☆

A man was lugging a grandfather clock from an antique shop to his car, three blocks away. Swaggering with each step, unable to see directly in front of him, he accidentally bumped an elderly couple heading in his direction on the sidewalk.

"I'm so sorry," he apologized, turning awkwardly toward them.

The couple glared at him angrily. The lady snapped, "Why don't you wear a wristwatch, like everyone else?"

☆ ☆ ☆

A lonely frog telephoned the Psychic Hotline and asked what his future held. He was told, "You are going to meet a beautiful young girl who wants to know everything about you."

"That's great. Where do I meet her?" he asked.

"In a biology lab."

In a *Peanuts* cartoon, Lucy says, "If you don't tell me you love me, I'm going to hold my breath until I pass out."

Schroeder looks up from his piano and says, "Breath-holding children are an interesting phenomenon. It could indicate a metabolic disorder. You probably need Vitamin B6. You should eat more beef liver."

Lucy sighs. "I ask for love, and all I get is beef liver."

☆ ☆ ☆

"How'd you enjoy the county fair?" Grandma asked.

"Waste of time," reported Jennifer. "It was so small, it only had one bumper car."

☆ ☆ ☆

A young Indian brave requested a meeting with the chief of his tribe.

"Oh, great chief, I understand that you name each child in our tribe," the brave began.

"That is true," the chief replied.

"Great chief, would you explain to me how you choose each name?" the brave continued.

The chief bowed his head for a moment, and responded, "When the news comes to me that a child has been born to our tribe, I bow my head in silent thanksgiving. When I look up, the first sight my eyes behold becomes the name of the child. If I see a deer running by, the child is named Running Deer. If I see snowflakes in the air, the child is named Snow Gently Falling.

"So, Dying Dog, why do you ask?"

Two English tourists in France walked past a towering statue of Napoleon. As they did, a squirrel hiding under one of the statue's ears tossed a nutshell fragment at the humans below. It landed lightly against the ear of one of them.

He brushed his ear and glared up at the statue, but failed to see the squirrel, or anything else that could have bombed him from above. "I do believe that statue spat at me," he told his companion.

"Well, I must say," intoned the other dryly, "it does seem to be a spitting image of the old boy."

☆　☆　☆

A professor perfected the art of cloning. He called a press conference to unveil his most prestigious work. He had taken cells from his own body and created a perfect clone of himself. After describing his work, he brought out his clone. The crowd of scientists and scientific journalists was astonished. The clone was a mirror image of the professor.

The professor asked the clone to speak. The clone soon became abusive and started spewing obscenities. When the embarrassed professor tried to intervene, a fight broke out between the two. The professor got the upper hand on his clone and in one last knockout punch sent him crashing through the window of the tenth story auditorium. The clone fell to his death.

The police were called and promptly arrested the professor. The charge: Making an obscene clone fall.

One of the sideshows at the circus featured a strong man who squeezed an orange until it was completely dry. When he finished, the strong man's manager challenged anybody in the audience to come forward and try to get one last drop of juice out of the super-compressed piece of fruit. To make the offer a bit more enticing, the manager offered a thousand dollars to anyone who successfully eked out even one tiny drop of juice.

A weight lifter with bulging muscles bounded up onto the stage, grabbed the orange from the manager, and pressed it with all his might. Nothing came out. Next a big, burly construction worker sauntered up and took his turn. After ten minutes of intense squeezing and a lot of grimacing, the construction worker finally admitted defeat.

"Any other takers?" the manager asked with a satisfied sneer.

"May I try?" responded a short, skinny, bespectacled man from the back row.

The manager couldn't keep a straight face as he and the rest of the crowd watched the stranger make his way up to the front. But the laughter suddenly stopped when, to everyone's amazement, the little guy picked up the orange and squeezed a puddle of juice onto the floor.

Flabbergasted, the manager sputtered, "How in the world did you do that?"

"I'm with the IRS," the man replied.

I had a terrible time. First off I got tonsillitis, followed by appendicitis and pneumonia. After that, I got rheumatism, and to top it off they gave me hypodermics and inoculations. I thought I would never get through that spelling bee.

☆ ☆ ☆

"This," said the pharmacist, "is guaranteed to make hair start growing back within a week."

He handed a jar of cream over to a balding customer for examination.

"Works in less than a week, you say?" the man asked.

"As advertised," the pharmacist assured him.

The customer opened the jar, touched a bit of the cream to his finger, reached across the counter and rubbed it on the pharmacist's own bald spot. "I'll be back in a week," he said, "to see if you're telling the truth."

☆ ☆ ☆

A Philadelphia law firm sent flowers to an associate firm in Baltimore upon the opening of its new offices. Through some mixup, the ribbon on the floral arrangement read "Deepest Sympathy." When the florist was informed of his mistake, he let out a cry of alarm. "Good heavens," he exclaimed, "then the flowers that went to the funeral said, 'Congratulations on Your New Location!'"

A seaman meets a pirate in a bar, and talk turns to their adventures on the sea. The seaman notes that the pirate has a peg leg, a hook, and an eye patch.

The seaman asks, "So, how did you end up with the peg leg?"

The pirate replies, "We was in a storm at sea, and I was swept overboard into a school of sharks. Just as me men were pulling me out, a shark bit me leg off."

"Wow!" said the seaman. "What about your hook?"

"Well," replied the pirate, "we was boardin' an enemy ship and battlin' the other sailors with swords. One of the enemy cut me hand off."

"Incredible!" remarked the seaman. "How did you get the eye-patch?"

"A seagull feather floated into me eye," replied the pirate.

"You lost your eye to a seagull feather?" the sailor asked incredulously.

"Well," said the pirate, "it was me first day with the hook."

☆ ☆ ☆

A man who had always dreamed of owning a Cadillac finally became the proud owner of his dream car, but only a short time before his untimely demise. He was so enamored of his car that he added a codicil to his will asking to be buried in it. This request was honored. A suitable grave was prepared, and the Cadillac was lowered down a ramp with the remains of the proud owner inside. Two boys watched with amazement. One exclaimed, "Boy, that's what I call living!"

"I hear Sam Culpepper passed away last week."

"Yeah, he was right well off, too. I'd like to know how much property he left."

" 'Bout all of it, I expect."

☆　☆　☆

Jones was a notorious tightwad, and alleviated his few twinges of conscience by giving a quarter to the miserable-looking woman who sold bagels from a pushcart on the corner near his office. He never bought a bagel, having already breakfasted, but he always put a quarter into her grimy palm and felt himself a virtuous man.

This went on for months, until one day the bagel-seller tugged at his immaculate cuff. "Mister, Mister, I gotta tell ya somethin'."

"Ah," acknowledged Jones with a gracious smile, "I suppose you wish to know why I give you a quarter every day but never take the bagel?"

"Nah, that's yer business," she snorted. "My business is tellin' ya the price's gone up to thirty-five cents."

☆　☆　☆

A woman paid $50 to a palm reader. "I'm in a crisis," she explained hurriedly. "Can you predict the next four or five months?"

"Certainly," replied the shyster, pocketing the money. "March, April, May, June, and July. For another twenty bucks, I'll take you to the end of the year."

The successful novelist, being interviewed on a TV talk show, confessed to burnout and self-doubt. "After twelve books and $8 million dollars in royalties, I finally realize I haven't the slightest talent for writing. Every one of my plots is just a rehash of things I've read by other writers."

"Are you telling us," hazarded the host, "that you're retiring?"

"Oh, of course not! Imagine what that would do to my reputation!"

☆ ☆ ☆

A Chicago executive on business in Mississippi wanted to write an E-mail to his wife back home, who was planning to join him the next day. The man couldn't quite remember her E-mail address, so he typed in an address as best he could remember.

Unfortunately, the address was that of the widow of a recently departed minister. The grieving woman, noticing that she had mail, opened the message and began to read:

"Dear Honey, I have arrived here safely. Everything is prepared for your arrival tomorrow. All my love. P.S.: By the way, bring a fan, cause it sure is hot down here!"

☆ ☆ ☆

A New York cab driver said with unrealized candor, "It's not the work that I enjoy so much as the people I run into."

Prayer

Two men were discussing how much they knew about religion, each boasting he knew more than the other. Finally, to prove his superiority, one said, "I bet you can't say the Lord's Prayer."

"Well, I'll just take that bet," the other man said. "Now I lay me down to sleep," he proudly proclaimed.

The challenger looked at him in amazement and said, "I didn't think you knew it."

✩ ✩ ✩

Bill Moyers served as press secretary to President Lyndon Johnson, who referred to him as "my Baptist preacher" and often called on him to "give thanks for the meal." On one occasion, the president, who was having difficulty hearing, interrupted him in the middle of his prayer. "Louder, Bill! I can't hear you."

Moyers replied, "I wasn't talking to you, Mr. President."

Two Midwest towns a few miles from each other maintained a friendly but pronounced rivalry over the years. One one occasion, the mayor of Town A visited the mayor of Town B, at a time when a crisis was erupting.

The mayor of Town B picked up the telephone and called the Lord for a decision. "Do you do that often?" the visiting mayor asked. "Oh, yes," the other answered. "Whenever I'm uncertain what to do, I give Him a call and receive the solution to my problem. You can do the same. Here's His number.

A month later, the mayor of Town A called the neighboring mayor. "I've been calling the Lord's number, as you suggested," he said. "And the results are good. But I just got a giant phone bill that's going to ruin my budget. How do you handle that?"

"Oh, I forgot to tell you," the mayor of Town B said. "From here, it's a local call."

☆ ☆ ☆

The little boy's parents told him he couldn't go to the picnic because he had been naughty. After a while, they forgave him and told him he could go. He began to cry.

They asked him what was wrong and he told them, "It's too late. I already prayed for rain."

"Lord," came the prayer, "so far, so good. I haven't sworn today, stolen anything, boasted, gotten angry at anyone, or even had any evil thoughts.

"But now comes the test, and I implore your help. I have to get up and go to work. . . ."

☆ ☆ ☆

A little boy ended a lengthy prayer that had included everyone he could think of by saying: "And Dear God, take care of yourself. If anything happens to you, we're all sunk."

☆ ☆ ☆

A pastor said the best prayer he ever heard was: "Lord, please make me the kind of person my dog thinks I am."

☆ ☆ ☆

She sowed her wild oats and then prayed for a crop failure!

☆ ☆ ☆

A small child was heard reciting the Lord's Prayer: "Forgive us our trash passes as we forgive those who pass trash against us."

Presidents

An American president once called a break from a long Cabinet meeting and strolled onto the White House lawn to gather his thoughts. He placed a hand on a garden rail and stood staring across the grass. For five full minutes, the president didn't move a muscle.

"He's really torn by this one," one Cabinet official said quietly to another. "I've never before seen him this deep in thought."

Another five minutes passed, and the nation's highest officials looked on nervously as the president continued to stand perfectly still.

Eventually, the chief executive motioned for his Cabinet to gather around him at the rail. "See that squirrel out there?" he asked, pointing. "It hasn't flinched for more than ten minutes. I do believe it's dead."

Abraham Lincoln assembled his Cabinet to seek their advice about a matter. After some discussion, he called for a vote. As he polled the group, each Cabinet member voted "aye." Then Lincoln said, "I vote 'nay' and the nays have it."

☆ ☆ ☆

Franklin Roosevelt saw a sign in a military facility he was visiting that read, "Illumination must be extinguished when the premises are vacated." He asked them to change it to, "Turn out the lights when you leave."

Problem Solving

Three engineers—electrical, chemical, and software—are traveling in a car, when suddenly, the vehicle just stops by the side of the road. The three engineers look at each other, wondering what could be wrong.

The electrical engineer suggests stripping down the electronics of the car and trying to trace where a fault might have occurred.

The chemical engineer suggests that perhaps the fuel has broken down and caused the problem.

The software engineer then offers his suggestion: "Why don't we close all the windows, get out, get back in, and open the windows again? Maybe it'll work!"

☆ ☆ ☆

A little boy from the city was visiting his cousins on the farm. Milking cows particularly fascinated him. "I think I see how you get it going," he told his uncle after watching intently. "But how do you turn it off?"

An elderly gentleman was a hopeless insomniac, and his wife and grown children at length resorted to taking him to a hypnotist. The hypnotist had a remarkable record for being able to cure such ailments—but his services were not cheap. "We'll pay whatever it costs," the mother declared. "Not only is he unable to rest himself, but he's depriving me of my rest, too."

The hypnotist proceeded as expected. He had the patient recline comfortably and then sat before him, slowly waving a gold pocket watch from a chain. He waited a few minutes before speaking at all, simply moving the watch in slow, precise arcs.

"You are becoming very, very drowsy," he began. "Your body is tired. . . . Your mind is tired. . . . Your muscles are weary. . . . You need rest. . . . Complete rest. . ."

This stage lasted for quite some time before the hypnotist got around to giving the instructions. "And now you must rest. You must sleep. Your family will take you home and put you into your warm, comfortable bed. You will sleep without waking for exactly eight hours. This you must do every night for a month, at the end of which time you will come back to see me and we will talk again about rest. . .rest. . .beautiful, peaceful rest."

Softer and softer the hypnotist's voice became. Finally, each member of the family sitting around the room was almost asleep. The victim himself had closed his eyes and was beginning to snore.

"You may take him home now," the hypnotist quietly advised, rousing the family. Ecstatic, they wrote a check for even more than the predetermined amount, and the hypnotist left the room.

The sons gently began to lift their father from the chair, whereupon he opened his eyes, glanced furtively around the room and asked, "Is that imbecile finally gone?"

☆　☆　☆

The little town had just acquired a state-of-the-art fire engine, and a debate warmed the next town council meeting over what to do with the venerable antique the new truck had replaced. Some wanted to sell fragments as souvenirs. Some wanted to display it in a museum. Some said it should be scrapped.

At length, grizzled volunteer Charlie stood and silenced the contenders. "I move we keep the old truck in service," he proposed. "Use it for false alarms."

Psychiatry

Doctor: "Our testing shows you're clearly schizophrenic. You have twin personalities."

Patient: "Yes, one of me sees that clearly. But the other me wants a second opinion."

☆ ☆ ☆

"Doctor, I just can't pull myself together."

"Sure you can. Now, sit right down and tell me precisely what your problem is."

"Well, you see, I'm a pair of curtains. . . ."

☆ ☆ ☆

Bridget: "You look worried."

Brodie: "I am. I'm convinced I'm losing my mind."

Bridget: "Nonsense! What makes you think so?"

Brodie: "Well, I heard that one person in five suffers from a mental disorder. My four sisters are all normal, so it must be me."

A psychiatrist prescribed a $90 bottle of pills and promised it would boost her patient's discernment and intelligence. A month later, the patient returned.

"Dr. Strathburn, I believe that medicine you prescribed is worthless. And I was very disturbed to learn you own stock in the drug company."

"See? You're wiser already."

☆ ☆ ☆

"Doc, I've been having horrible dreams at night."

"What are they about?"

"Well, last night I dreamed I was in a pasture eating grass with a herd of cows."

"That's odd, but not really problematic. Why does it bother you?"

"When I got up this morning, the corner of my bed was missing."

☆ ☆ ☆

"I'm so unhappy with myself," intoned a patient to her psychiatrist. "See those tomatoes growing in my hair?"

The psychiatrist decided to play along with the delusion for a moment. "Yes, I see. What's wrong with them?"

"Why, they represent yet another failure in my life."

"How do you mean?"

"I planted watermelons."

The young, bearded man sat in the psychiatrist's office clapping his hands in a steady but strange cadence: clap. . .clap-clap. . .clap. . .clap-clap. . .

When it came the young man's turn, the psychiatrist immediately asked him the meaning of the hand-clap routine.

"It's a secret ritual," the patient answered. "I learned it from a street musician."

"What's its purpose?"

"It keeps killer sharks away."

"Oh, you won't be bothered by a shark in here," assured the psychiatrist.

"Yes, I know," the patient replied, continuing to clap.

"So what seems to be your problem?"

"I think I'm going batty. I keep thinking it's Monday."

"This is Monday. You're cured. That'll be $50."

☆ ☆ ☆

Wendy found that her difficulty making even the simplest decisions was causing her problems on the job. Finally, she decided to seek professional help.

"Tell me, Wendy," the psychiatrist began gently, "I understand you have trouble making decisions. Is that so?"

Wendy's brow furrowed. "Well," she finally answered, "yes. . .and no."

Quotables

Preparation: "It wasn't raining when Noah built the ark." (Howard Ruff)

☆ ☆ ☆

Candid: "I don't want any yes-men around me. I want everybody to tell the truth, even if it costs them their jobs." (Samuel Goldwyn)

☆ ☆ ☆

Success: "By the time we've made it, we've had it." (Malcolm Forbes)

☆ ☆ ☆

Overpopulation: "Somewhere on this globe, every ten seconds there is a woman giving birth to a child. She must be found and stopped." (Sam Levenson)

Formula for a long life: "Keep breathing." (Sophie Tucker)

☆　☆　☆

Humor: "He who laughs, lasts." (Mary Poole)

☆　☆　☆

Gossip: "If you haven't got anything nice to say about anybody, come sit next to me." (Alice Roosevelt Longworth)

☆　☆　☆

Emotions: "The advantage of emotions is that they lead us astray." (Oscar Wilde)

☆　☆　☆

Fashion: "She wears her clothes as if they were thrown on her with a pitchfork. (Jonathan Swift)

☆　☆　☆

Attendance: "If people don't want to come out to the ballpark, nobody's going to stop them." (Yogi Berra)

Real Estate

A realtor was showing a lovely piece of retirement property to a sullen, bargain-minded couple. "Isn't that a spectacular view?" the realtor suggested, pointing across a sunlit valley of green.

"Hmph," said the man. "Apart from the mountains, what's there to see?"

☆　☆　☆

A rancher was gazing across the vast expanse of the Grand Canyon for the first time in his life. "That," he remarked, "would be a mighty tough place to recover stray cattle."

Restaurants

A diner shrieked when she saw a winged insect floating in her bowl of soup. "What's this?" she yelled at the waitress.

The waitress peered into the bowl. "I'd say it's either a small mosquito or a large gnat."

☆ ☆ ☆

Joy: "Why don't we try the King's Palace for dinner? I've heard they have fabulous seafood entrees."
Walt: "Nah, nobody eats there anymore. It's too crowded. . . ."

☆ ☆ ☆

Diner: "Would you please bring me some water?"
Waitress: "To drink?"
Diner: "No, actually, I thought I might take a bath."

Stranger in Town: "How's the food at the Main Street Diner?"

Resident: "Well, it's kinda greasy, but a lot of locals go there because they can eat dirt cheap."

Stranger: "That's good—except I don't much care for dirt."

☆ ☆ ☆

One hotel coffee shop in Niagara Falls has the perfect salad for newlyweds: lettuce alone!

☆ ☆ ☆

A man came into a delicatessen and ordered a meal, but warned the waiter, "I love bread. I don't care about the rest of the meal, but I want to have a lot of fresh bread."

The waiter left, returning a few minutes later with a salad and a straw basket with two pieces of bread. The customer started to eat, but asked for more bread.

When he served the soup, the waiter put four pieces of bread in the straw basket. The customer gulped down the soup and chewed up all the bread, so the waiter brought eight more slices with the main course. Before he started eating his entree, the customer ate all the bread. Seeing the empty basket, the waiter took a foot-long loaf of bread, sliced it lengthwise, and brought it over to the table. The customer took one look and said, "Why'd you go back to two slices?"

A man walked into a restaurant and said, "I'd like a plate of stew and a kind word." When the waitress returned with the man's meal and set it down in front of him, he whispered, "How about the kind word?"

"Don't eat the stew," the waitress replied.

✩ ✩ ✩

A waiter brought a customer the steak he had ordered. His thumb was on the meat.

"What's the matter with you?" yelled the customer. "Why have you got your hand all over my steak?"

"You don't want it to fall on the floor again, do you?"

✩ ✩ ✩

A man entered a restaurant on the banks of the Chesapeake Bay, sat down, and began looking rather impatient and grouchy. At last a waiter appeared.

"It's about time!" said the man. "Now tell me. Do you serve crabs here?"

"Certainly sir," replied the waiter. "We serve anyone."

✩ ✩ ✩

After a delicious lunch in a New York Italian restaurant, a businesswoman called the chef to compliment him on the meal. "Frankly, your eggplant parmesan was better than the one I ate in Milan last week," she told him.

"That's not surprising," the chef said. "They use domestic cheese. I use only imported."

Did you hear about the new restaurant that just opened up on the moon?

Good food, but no atmosphere.

☆ ☆ ☆

A woman seated in an exclusive restaurant ordered caviar. "And please make sure that it's imported," she said, "because I can't tell the difference."

☆ ☆ ☆

Two men finished a meal and looked at the check put down by the waiter. One man said, "Let's split the check. You wash, I'll dry!"

☆ ☆ ☆

A man wandered into a run-down restaurant and started talking to the man sweeping the floor. "I can't understand it," he said. "You work in a dump like this?"

"At least I don't eat here," the janitor snapped.

School

Mother: "How are you doing in math?"
Child: "I can handle some of the digits."
Mother: "What do you mean?"
Child: "The whole numbers are a bit of a bother, but I
can figure the zeros correctly every time!"

☆ ☆ ☆

A father looked on as his wife signed their son's report
card. "Why are you signing each page with an X?" he
asked.

"You don't want his teachers to think anybody who's
literate has a sixth-grader like that, do you?"

☆ ☆ ☆

Teacher: "What do you get when you multiply 63
times 14?"
Albert: "The wrong answer, I'm sure."

The fifth-grader was having so much trouble with his math homework that he finally had to call in his father for assistance. The next morning, he confidently turned the assignment in to his teacher.

Imagine his amazement when the paper was returned at the end of the day with a grade of 60 and a big red F at the top of the page.

"Hey!" the boy cried, rising from his desk. "You've flunked my Dad!"

☆　☆　☆

"What are algebraic symbols for?" a sixth-grader asked her high-school sister.

"That's how the math teacher talks when he can't express himself in plain English."

☆　☆　☆

The father of a high school senior phoned the Latin teacher and demanded to know why his son had been given an F on the mid-year exam.

"Because we're not allowed to give a G," said the teacher.

☆　☆　☆

Each year, the teacher sent home a note with every child which read, "Dear Parents, if you promise not to believe everything your child says happens at school, I'll promise not to believe everything he or she says happens at home."

Biology Teacher: "As you can see from these diagrams, there are thousands of miles of arteries, veins, and capillaries in the human body."

Student: "I guess that's why old people have 'tired blood.' "

☆　☆　☆

Teacher: "What is twenty-four times eight?"

Pupil: "One hundred ninety-two."

Teacher: "That's very good."

Pupil: "Whaddya mean, very good? It's absolutely perfect."

☆　☆　☆

"Mark, can you give us an example of a double negative?" the English teacher asked.

Mark rubbed his chin and slowly shook his head. "I can't think of no double negatives."

☆　☆　☆

Donny came home from school one afternoon and, as required, handed his mother a discipline ticket the teacher had given him.

"Now, Donny, what did you do to get a discipline ticket?"

"I really dunno, Mom. Marv and Ellie were talking to me in science class, and the next thing I knew, I got caught."

A father was reviewing his daughter's report card with disapproval. "You don't seem to be working very hard," he commented.

"I work as hard as anybody else in class," she snapped.

"Well, your teacher doesn't seem very impressed."

"How do you expect us to impress somebody who's earned a master's degree?"

☆　☆　☆

A high school student came home from school seeming rather depressed.

"What's the matter, son?" asked his mother.

"It's my grades. They're all wet."

"What do you mean 'all wet'?"

"They're below C-level," he replied.

☆　☆　☆

A young girl said to her friend after a spelling test, "Sure, I know how to spell banana—I just don't know when to stop."

☆　☆　☆

A little girl complained that she didn't want to go back to school.

"But why, Jenny?" asked her mother.

"Well, I can't read. I can't write, and they won't let me talk."

The teacher noticed that Milton was staring out the window and not paying attention to the classroom discussion.

Wanting to make an example of him, the teacher said, quite loudly and sharply, "Milton, what is your opinion of the question we're discussing?"

"Oh, I'm sorry, sir," Milton replied. "I didn't hear you. I was lost in thought."

"Well," said the teacher, "I'm not surprised you were lost. I realize it's unfamiliar territory."

✫ ✫ ✫

When Abraham Lincoln was a lad in school, he was known for being a good speller. One day a classmate was asked to spell the word "defied." She was intimidated by the stern schoolteacher, and uncertain whether the word contained a "y" or "i" in the middle. But she noticed Lincoln smiling at her and pointing to his eye.

"D-e-f-i-e-d," she spelled correctly.

✫ ✫ ✫

On the first day of school, a freckle-faced lad handed his new teacher a note from his mother. The teacher unsealed the note, read it, looked at the child with a frown and placed the note inside a desk drawer.

"So what did she write?" the boy asked.

"It's a disclaimer."

"A what?"

"It says, 'The opinions expressed by Leo are not necessarily those of his mother and father.' "

353

A teacher asked, "What did Paul Revere say at the end of his famous ride?"

A student answered, "Whoa!"

☆ ☆ ☆

"Jim, where's your lunch box?" the teacher asked.

"Oh, I ain't got none. I'm eating in the cafeteria."

"No, no, Jim. You say, 'I don't have a lunch box. You don't have a lunch box. Sally doesn't have one. We don't have any.' "

Jim looked puzzled. "So, what happened to all the lunch boxes?"

☆ ☆ ☆

The regularly tardy high school student ran into geometry class a minute after the bell rang, slamming the door behind him. He noisily collapsed into his desk and slammed his book bag to the floor.

"Ken, what kind of behavior is that?" the teacher demanded. "You've distracted everybody. You know you should walk in school, not run."

"But you told me last week I'd be suspended if I walked into your class late one more time."

☆ ☆ ☆

History Teacher: "Why was Washington standing in the bow of the boat as the army crossed the Delaware?"
Student: "Because he knew if he sat down, he'd have to row."

A teacher caught a student chewing gum in class.

"Who gave you the gum?" the teacher asked.

"I don't remember."

"How long have you been chewing it?"

"Not very long."

"Haven't you been caught doing that before?"

"Now and then, I suppose."

"Okay, go stand in the corner."

The student was concerned, because the recess bell was about to ring. "How long do I have to stay here?"

The teacher smiled. "Just for awhile."

☆　☆　☆

"The word 'corpse' has an 'e' on the end," the teacher corrected a spelling student. "Don't you know the difference between a 'corps' and a 'corpse'?"

"I think so," the student answered. "A corps is a dead man, and a corpse is a dead woman."

☆　☆　☆

A first-grade teacher had instructed her students to draw examples of rings. She slowly walked around the room, examining their ideas. At Will's desk, she stopped in surprise.

"But Will," she said, "those are all squares and rectangles."

"No, they're not," Will protested. "They're boxing rings."

While waiting to enter the school lunchroom, a fifth-grader was ordered to the back of the line for rowdiness. A minute later, he resumed his old place.

"What are you trying to do?" asked the teacher monitoring the lunch line. "I sent you to the rear."

"I went, but there's already somebody back there."

☆ ☆ ☆

Early one morning, a mother wakened her son.

"Get up, son. It's time to go to school."

"But why, Mom? I don't want to go."

"Give me two reasons why you shouldn't go to school," his mother said.

"Well, for one, the kids hate me," he replied. "And the teachers hate me, too!"

"Oh, those aren't good reasons to stay home. Come on now and get ready," his mother coaxed.

"Give me two reasons why I *should* go to school," he demanded.

"Well, for one thing, you're 47 years old. And for another, you're the principal!"

☆ ☆ ☆

On the first day of school, the kindergarten teacher said, "If anyone has to go to the bathroom, hold up two fingers."

A little voice from the back of the room asked, "How will that help?"

Finding one of her students making faces at others on the playground, Ms. Smith stopped to gently reprove the child. Smiling sweetly the teacher said, "When I was a child, I was told if I made scary faces I would stay like that."

The student looked up and replied, "Well you can't say you weren't warned."

☆　☆　☆

Mother and Father were writing out payments for the monthly bills one evening.

"Electricity, credit card interest, groceries—everything is going up!" exclaimed the father.

"Nothing ever goes down," agreed the mom.

"Take a look at this!" chirped their child, entering the room with her report card.

Science

A traveler in Montana stopped at an isolated, weather-beaten store. Behind the cash register was a large, colorful chunk of petrified wood.

"I'd love to know how old a piece of wood like that is," remarked the traveler.

"It's exactly two million and fourteen years old," said the grizzled proprietor.

"How can you be so precise?"

"A geology professor stopped in here and told me it was a two-million-year-old rock. That was fourteen years ago."

☆ ☆ ☆

"I have just developed the most powerful acid compound known to humans," a scientist announced to her colleagues. "There is only one problem."

"What is that?" asked one.

"Finding a container for it."

If evolution holds true, why hasn't nature produced a housewife who can vacuum the floor, answer the phone, help with the homework, and change the baby all at the same time? And why hasn't it produced a pedestrian who can dodge three vehicles at once?

☆ ☆ ☆

When Albert Einstein was asked to explain how radio waves worked, he said: "You see, wire telegraph is a kind of very long cat. You pull his tail in New York and his head is meowing in Los Angeles. And radio operates exactly the same way, only there is no cat."

☆ ☆ ☆

"Every inanimate object on the face of the earth falls into either of two categories," an engineering professor proposed in a lecture. "One, they are objects that immediately require fixing, or two, they are objects that require fixing after humans have tinkered with them."

☆ ☆ ☆

Two laboratory white mice were discussing their situation.

"It's not so bad," commented one. "A few of these humans are actually rather intelligent."

"Which ones are you talking about?"

"That Dr. Autrey, for example. I think I have her quite trained. Whenever I'm hungry, I press a button that turns on a little red light bulb. Presto! She appears out of nowhere and gives me a piece of cheese."

Albert Einstein was making the rounds of the lecture circuit, but he found himself longing to get back to his laboratory work. One night, as he was riding to yet another rubber-chicken dinner, Einstein mentioned to his chauffeur (a man who somewhat resembled the famous scientist in looks and manner) that he was tired of making speeches. "I have an idea, boss," his chauffeur said. "I've heard you give this speech so many times, I'll bet I could give it for you."

Einstein laughed out loud and said, "Why not? Let's do it!"

When they arrived at the dinner, Einstein donned the chauffeur's cap and jacket and sat in the back of the room, while the driver took Einstein's place at the head table. After the meal, the chauffeur gave a beautiful rendition of Einstein's speech, and even answered a few questions expertly.

Then a supremely pompous professor stood up and asked an extremely esoteric question about antimatter formation, digressing here and there to let everyone in the audience know that he was nobody's fool.

Without missing a beat, the chauffeur fixed the professor with a steely stare and said, "Sir, the answer to that question is so simple that I'll bet even my chauffeur, who is sitting in the back of the room, can answer it."

Two molecules are walking down the street and run in to each other. One says to the other, "Are you all right?"

"No, I lost an electron!"

"Are you sure?"

"I'm positive!"

Sermons

"Prepare to meet your Maker. Every single member of this congregation is going to die," thundered the minister to the people one Sunday. "What's so funny?" he asked one man who seemed to enjoy his stern words.

"I'm not a member of this congregation," the man answered.

✫ ✫ ✫

After the service, the minister said to a woman, "I noticed that your husband walked out during the sermon. Did I say something he didn't like?"

"No," she replied, "but he does have a bad habit of sleepwalking."

✫ ✫ ✫

The sermon was endless. Getting to another point, the minister said, "What else can I say?"

A member of the congregation yelled out, "Amen!"

"Your sermon was simply superb," gushed a woman at the church door. Then added, "I hope it will be printed."

The minister answered, "Thank you. I'll have it printed posthumously."

"Oh, that's wonderful," she went on, "and the sooner the better."

✩　✩　✩

A minister asked the chairman of the flower committee what was done with the Sunday flowers. She replied, "We give them to the people who are sick after the sermon."

✩　✩　✩

Now once upon a time, and not so very long ago
　A preacher preaching to his flock observed with spirit low
　　That half his congregation sat a-dozing in the pews
　　A strange locale it seemed to him to take a weekly snooze.
　　However, a resourceful man, and always in the groove,
　　　He bought a tape recorder, his orations to improve,
　　　And a stimulating sermon he proceeded to record
　　　Then played it back to find the reasons why his flock was bored.
　　　And when his wife came in she heard a dissertation deep
　　　And found the speaker in his chair relaxed and sound asleep.

Said the minister from the pulpit: "I do not mind too much when, during my sermon, some of you cast covert glances at your watches. What does upset me is when you hold your watches next to your ears to make sure they are still running."

☆ ☆ ☆

At the conclusion of the sermon, the worshipers filed out of the sanctuary to greet the minister. As one of them left, he shook the minister's hand, thanked him for the sermon and said, "Thanks for the message, Reverend. You know, you must be smarter than Einstein."

Beaming with pride, the minister said, "Why, thank you, brother!"

As the week went by, the minister began to think about the man's compliment. The more he thought, the more he became baffled as to why anyone would deem him smarter than Einstein. So he decided to ask the man the following Sunday.

The next Sunday he asked the parishioner if he remembered the previous Sunday's comment about the sermon. The parishioner replied that he did. The minister asked: "Exactly what did you mean that I must be smarter than Einstein?"

The man replied, "Well, Reverend, they say that Einstein was so smart that only ten people in the entire world could understand him. But Reverend, no one can understand you."

The minister had so thoroughly bored the members of his congregation that they finally asked him to leave. "Give me one more chance," he pleaded.

The congregation turned out in force the next Sunday and heard him deliver, to their surprise and delight, the most inspired sermon they'd heard in years. After the service, everyone shook his hand warmly. One man, an elder of the church, said, "You must stay, with an increase in salary, of course."

The minister accepted. Then the elder said, "That was the greatest sermon I have ever heard. But tell me one thing. As you began to speak, you raised two fingers of your left hand. When you were done, you raised two fingers of your right hand. What was the significance of those gestures?"

"Those," answered the minister, "were the quotation marks."

✩ ✩ ✩

A minister told his congregation, "To prepare your hearts for next Sunday's sermon, I want you all to read Mark 17 sometime this week."

The following Sunday, as he prepared to deliver his sermon, the minister asked for a show of hands. "How many of you read Mark 17 this week?"

Every hand went up.

The minister smiled and said, "The book of Mark has only sixteen chapters. Which brings us to this morning's sermon: 'The Sin of Lying.' "

Someone wrote a letter to the editor of a London paper saying that he had gone to church for about fifty years, listened to about twenty-five hundred sermons, each of which had probably taken about ten hours to write. He concluded, "That is about twenty-five thousand hours of professional time. And, to tell you the truth, I can only remember one or two of them. I think the minister's time would be better spent on something else."

A few days later, a letter in reply appeared from a person who said he had also gone to church about fifty years, but he looked at the matter differently. He said, "I've also been married about fifty years and my wife has made three meals a day for me, about one thousand a year, about fifty thousand during the time we have been married. I can only remember one or two of them, but they all did me good, nourished me and kept me alive, and gave me strength to keep going."

☆ ☆ ☆

A minister made his way through a blizzard one Sunday to a little church out in the range country of the west. Only one man showed up and the minister wondered if they should go ahead with the service. The man said: "I'm a rancher. I don't know anything about preaching, but I do know this—if only one cow shows up, I feed it." So the preacher proceeded with a full service and sermon. Afterward, his single attendee voiced a further opinion, "I don't know anything about preaching, but I do know this—if only one cow shows up, I don't dump the whole load."

A minister visited a large, flourishing church to see why it was so popular. He discovered that the minister used a story whenever the interest of the congregation began to sag. For instance, on the day he visited he heard the minister shock the congregation into attention by announcing: "Some of the best hours of my life have been spent in the arms of another man's wife." Then he added: "And I'm going to confess to you who that was."

The interest was so intense they hardly dared breathe as they waited for the revelation. The minister told them: "That woman was my mother."

Thought the visiting minister, "Ah, I've got just what I need," as he went back to his church to put the new-found ploy into play. When interest dropped, as it regularly did, he startled them by saying: "Some of the happiest hours of my life have been spent in the arms of another man's wife." Then, with rapt attention from his audience, he paused and paused and finally blurted out: "But for the life of me, I can't remember who it was."

☆ ☆ ☆

"How do you know what to say?" a little boy asked his father who was working on a sermon.

"God tells me," the clergyman replied.

"Then why do you keep crossing things out?"

"Recently I've had complaints that my sermons are too intellectual," a minister announced during the service. "That being the case, the following adults are invited to come up for the children's sermon."

☆ ☆ ☆

A New Englander, fresh out of seminary, got his first pastorate in rural Kentucky. For his first Sunday, he prepared a powerful message on the evils of gambling, and delivered it superbly. Afterwards, the head deacon pulled the minister aside to say, "I should warn you, pastor, that many members of our congregation raise horses or feed that are used in the Kentucky Derby."

The next Sunday, the young pastor preached a powerful message on the evils of smoking. Once again, the head deacon warned the pastor, "I should tell you that many of our members have tobacco farms."

On the minister's third Sunday, he preached a powerful sermon on the evils of drinking. And once again, the head deacon pronounced a warning: "Pastor, you should know that many of our members have stills in their backyards."

The pastor began to wonder what sermon topic would not alienate a large percentage of his congregation. He thought over the matter until Thursday, when he had a revelation. That Sunday, he preached a powerful message on the evils of fishing in another nation's territorial waters.

COMMENTS BY PARISHIONERS
ON THE WAY OUT OF CHURCH:

"I don't care what others say, I think your sermons are all right."

"You always seem to find something to say."

"Did you know there are eighty-seven panes of glass in our windows?"

Shipshape

A man exercising on the promenade deck noticed that a lady was offering him a charming smile whenever he passed her deck chair. He arranged to sit at her table for dinner, and a good time was had by all. "You remind me of my third husband," she said.

"Oh, how often have you been married?" he asked.

Her reply: "Twice."

☆ ☆ ☆

A small child on an ocean liner slipped and fell overboard. Before his mother could call for help, a man flew over the rail, into the water, and saved the child.

As the hero was hoisted back onto the deck to the cheers of the other passengers, the captain said, "That was an amazing rescue. What can we do for you?"

"You can tell me who pushed me overboard," the man replied.

Once upon a time, there was a famous and very success-ful sea captain. For years, he guided merchant ships all over the world, and never once did stormy seas or pirates get the best of him. He was admired by his crew and fellow captains alike.

Every morning, he went through a strange ritual. He would lock himself in his captain's quarters and open a small safe. In the safe was an envelope with a piece of paper inside. He would stare at the paper for a minute, then lock it back up and go about his daily duties.

For years, this went on, and his crew became very curious. Was it a treasure map? A letter from a long-lost love? Everyone speculated about the contents of the envelope.

One day, the captain died. After burying his body at sea, the first mate led the entire crew into the captain's quarters, where he opened the safe, pulled out the envelope, opened the folded sheet of paper and read, "Port Left, Starboard Right."

☆ ☆ ☆

There was a young man from Ostend
    Who vowed he'd hold out till the end.
But when halfway over
    From Calais to Dover,
He did what he didn't intend!

A passenger asked the ship's physician for relief from sea-sickness, and the doctor assured him that no one ever died from this malady. "Please don't tell me that, Doctor," the man said. "The hope of dying is the only thing that's keeping me alive."

Signs

Optometrist: If you don't see what you're looking for, you've come to the right place.

Travel: Go away, please.

Plumber: A straight flush beats a full house.

Plumber: Don't sleep with a drip tonight, call a plumber.

Hospital: "The first five minutes of life can be the most risky." Handwritten underneath: "The last five minutes ain't so hot either."

Shoe Repair: We bring back departed soles.

Bumper sticker: Pass with care. Driver chews tobacco.

Tow Truck: We don't want an arm and a leg, just all of your tows.

Estate: Trespassers will be prosecuted to the full extent of the law. Sisters of Mercy.

Dry Cleaners: Thirty-seven years on the same spot.

School Cafeteria: "Shoes are required to eat in the cafeteria." Handwritten underneath: "Socks can eat wherever they like."

Funeral Home: Drive carefully. We can wait.

In a church parking lot: Reserved for the pastor. You park here, you preach.

Soldiers and Sailors

A rural mail carrier at the end of World War II took the news of the armistice to an isolated mountain family. He thought the good tidings would bring smiles, but the woman on the porch shook her head sadly.

"I s'pose it figures," she grumbled.

"What do you mean?" asked the carrier.

"We sent our Jeb off to join the army two months ago. That boy never could hold a job."

☆ ☆ ☆

A class of paratrooper recruits took the air on their first free-fall jump. At the designated altitude, they opened their chutes—but one late jumper streaked past them, the handle of the ripcord loose in his hand.

"Hey, are you okay?" shouted a shocked comrade.

"So far," came the reply.

A naval drill instructor was talking to new enlistees. "Now this is a dangerous maneuver, so you'd better listen slowly to what I'm about to tell you."

Whispered one recruit to another, "And what happens if we listen fast?"

☆   ☆   ☆

In the late 1940s, a veteran of World War II applied for a bank job. During the interview, the unsmiling, no-nonsense bank official fired question after question, taking notes and never glancing up at the veteran.

"Most recent job position?" was the question.

"Supply officer," the applicant replied.

"Duration of employment?"

"Three and a half years."

"Reason for termination?"

The applicant thought about it a moment and then answered, "We won the war."

☆   ☆   ☆

What did the frightened soldier do when a land mine tore up the main road?

He tore up a side path.

☆   ☆   ☆

"We received our uniforms today," a recruit wrote to his mother from boot camp. "It made me feel very proud, although the pants are a little too loose around the chest."

An army unit on training maneuvers hacked through heavy underbrush to the edge of a river. "Have you found a shallow place for us to cross over?" the lieutenant asked the platoon scout.

"Yes sir, about a hundred yards downstream."

The soldiers were exhausted when they made their way to the crossing point. Wading into the stream, they soon dropped into a deep hole. The whole platoon floundered in the current, gasping for breath.

"I thought you said this place was shallow!" the officer sputtered.

"Well, sir, I watched the ducks go all the way across, and it only came up to the tops of their legs."

☆　☆　☆

A young soldier was learning to parachute. He was given the following instructions:

(a) jump when you are told;

(b) count to ten and pull the ripcord:

(c) in the very unlikely event that it doesn't open, pull the second chute open;

(d) when you get down, a truck will take you back to the base.

When the plane had reached the proper altitude, the men started peeling out. The soldier jumped when told. He counted ten and pulled the cord, but the chute failed to open. He proceeded to the backup plan, pulling the cord of the second chute. It too, failed to open. "This is just great," he complained. "And when I get down, the truck probably won't be there either."

The story is told of a Civil War unit on patrol who'd lived on miserable hardtack for days. The soldiers were naturally excited when they spied a chicken on the road ahead of them. One of the privates broke and ran after the chicken.

"Halt!" shouted his lieutenant.

The soldier kept running.

"Halt, I say!" the officer repeated, angered by this display of insubordination.

The private pressed his pursuit of the chicken.

"Halt or I'll shoot!" the lieutenant cried, drawing his pistol.

Just at that moment, the soldier caught the chicken, snapped its neck and began toting it back toward his comrades. "I'll teach you to halt when the lieutenant orders you to halt!" he chided his newfound meal.

☆ ☆ ☆

Morgan: "My great-great-great-grandfather fought with General Custer."

Mitchum: "I don't doubt it. Your family'll fight any-body."

☆ ☆ ☆

Recruiting Officer: "What do you mean you want to join the army? You're still in high school. You're practically an infant!"

Teenager: "Yes, sir. I'd like to join the infantry."

An army troop had been on patrol more than a week. The soldiers were smelly and filthy.

One morning an order came down the ranks for them to change socks. "But we don't have any clean socks," said one of the men.

"Colonel's orders," said the sergeant. "He insists on cleanliness in the field. We all have to change socks."

The soldiers looked at each other, bewildered. After a minute, one of them had an idea. "Okay, Jefferson, you change with me. Bilinsky, you change with Carmichael. . . ."

☆ ☆ ☆

During a combat tactics course, a first sergeant asked a private, "Smith, what would you do if a thousand enemy soldiers were attacking from your front?"

Smith responded, "I'd gun them all down with my rifle."

The sergeant then asked, "And what if another five hundred enemy soldiers appeared to your right?"

"I'd gun them all down with my rifle, too," Smith answered.

"What if you turned to see another seven hundred enemy soldiers to your left?"

"I'd blast them with my rifle, too, sergeant."

After this third reply, the sergeant thundered, "Smith! Where are you getting all those bullets?!"

Smith replied, "The same place you're dredging up all those enemy soldiers!"

A general was inspecting a line of recruits. "Where ya from, son?" he asked one lad.

"Pennsylvania, sir!" barked the nervous soldier.

"Which part?"

"Uh—all of me, sir!"

✰ ✰ ✰

Feeling the helplessness that comes with seasickness the young sailor told another new sailor, "I knew I was a landlubber, but until now, I didn't know how much I lubbed it!"

Speakers

"What are we going to do to keep him from talking too long?" the people asked each other as they planned the retirement dinner for one of their long-winded colleagues. They decided to let him know that any speech that went on for more than six minutes would be gaveled to a halt.

When it came time for the honoree to respond at the end of the program, sure enough, he went on and on, just as everyone had feared. The master of ceremonies hesitated to do anything about it until he noticed the angry signals from the people that he should use the gavel. Finally he did, but in his nervousness, he pounded it on the head of the man next to him, instead of on the table.

As the man who was hit slid under the table, he was heard to say: "Hit me again—I can still hear him."

At a banquet that went on and on and on, the presiding officer of the club finally said, "Ladies and gentlemen, we have run considerably over time—but I am particularly pleased to introduce our distinguished keynote speaker, who will now give you his address."

The audience applauded, the speaker rose and said, "Mr. Toastmaster, ladies and gentlemen, my address is 239 East Thirty-eighth Street, New York City," and sat down.

The ballroom shook from the applause.

☆ ☆ ☆

After a lengthy and flowery introduction of the speaker, his little son was overheard saying: "I thought Dad was going to speak."

☆ ☆ ☆

An efficiency expert concluded his lecture with a note of caution. "You need to be careful about trying these techniques at home."

"Why?" asked somebody from the audience.

"I watched my wife's routine at breakfast for years," the expert explained. "She made lots of trips between the refrigerator, stove, table, and cabinets, often carrying a single item at a time. One day, I told her, 'Hon, why don't you try carrying several things at once?'"

"Did it save time?" the guy in the audience asked.

"Actually, yes," replied the expert. "It used to take her twenty minutes to make breakfast. Now I do it in seven."

As the speaker stood up to move to the rostrum, his wife handed him a piece of paper on which she had written "KISS." Upon completing his address, he returned to his seat and thanked his wife for the encouraging word she had sent up with him. She said, "I didn't mean 'kiss,' I meant 'Keep It Short, Stupid.' "

☆ ☆ ☆

When the speaker of the evening was introduced, with extravagant praises, at a banquet in his honor, he responded nervously: "You know, I came here in the hope of hearing a fascinating speech. I was hoping to hear my lips drip brilliant phrases and memorable epigrams. Now I have to tell you, I'm afraid I'm going to be disappointed."

☆ ☆ ☆

I love a finished speaker
    I really, really do.
I don't mean one who's polished
    I just mean one who's through.

☆ ☆ ☆

A person arrived a half-hour after a man started speaking at a town meeting in New England. He took a seat in the back and asked, in one of those whispers that sometimes carries throughout a room, "What's the speaker talking about?" He was told, in another whisper that carried to others, "He hasn't said yet."

George Bernard Shaw sent Winston Churchill two tickets to the opening night of his latest play with the note, "Here are two tickets. . .one for you and one for a friend. . .if you have one."

Churchill wrote back, "Thanks, but I can't make opening night. I'll come on the second night. . .if there is one."

Sports

Pepper Rodgers was having a bad season as coach of the UCLA football team. The fans and campus were turning against him. Even his wife and family were unhappy with the team. Only his dog stayed friendly and eager to see him. Pepper told his wife, "A man needs more than one friend, especially at a time of crisis." So she bought him another dog.

☆ ☆ ☆

Life isn't fair. When I tried out for baseball, I couldn't hit a curve. Now I play golf and I can't stop hitting them!

☆ ☆ ☆

Marge: "What inspired you to take up skydiving?"
Sue: "I was a passenger in a plane that ran out of gas at 5,000 feet."

"The X-ray shows a small spot under your kneecap, but it's probably just scar tissue," the doctor told the college quarterback. "I'm not very concerned about it."

The quarterback was not assured. "If it was your knee," he retorted, "I wouldn't be very concerned, either."

Head Coach: "That George is a slacker. He's so slow my grandmother could run him down."
Assistant Coach: "Well, there's one thing he does fast. Real fast. Faster'n anybody else on the team."
Head Coach: "What's that?"
Assistant Coach: "Get tired."

A losing pitcher approached his catcher outside the locker room. "Let me borrow a quarter," he said. "I promised one of my fans I'd phone him after the game."

The catcher searched his pockets. "I only have a dollar bill. Here, take it. Now you can phone all your fans."

A man explained his experience in a marathon. "I was running last. It was so embarrassing that even the guy in front of me, second to last, was making fun of me. He said, 'Hey, how does it feel to come in last?' I said, 'You want to know?' And I dropped out."

After a terrible half-inning, the pitcher came back to the dugout. Before sitting down, he kicked at the bat rack. The manager said, "Don't do that. You'll break your leg and we'll never be able to trade you."

☆ ☆ ☆

A college crew team had spent the whole afternoon rowing and were near exhaustion. Heading for the locker room, they were stopped by the team captain.

"Fellows, I have some good news and some bad news," he said. "The good news is you're to take a twenty-minute break, and then the college president is coming down here to watch you perform."

The rowers groaned. "So what's the bad news?" one asked sarcastically.

"He's bringing his water skis."

☆ ☆ ☆

"I like the statistics of your quarterback Evans," a pro scout told a college football coach. "What's your opinion of him personally?"

"Good skills. Sort of a prima donna, though."

"How do you mean?"

"Well, let's just say that when he makes a big play, he's a big advocate of the idea of taking personal responsibility for the way things happen. When he gets sacked, he's a big advocate of the concept of luck."

In the spring training, a rookie was asked the size of his cap. He said, "I don't know. I'm not in shape yet."

☆ ☆ ☆

A guy named Bob receives a free ticket to the Superbowl from his company. Unfortunately, when Bob arrives at the stadium he realizes the seat is in the last row in the corner of the stadium—he is closer to the Goodyear Blimp than the field.

About halfway through the first quarter, Bob notices an empty seat ten rows off the field right on the 50-yard line. He decides to take a chance and makes his way through the stadium and around the security guards to the empty seat.

As he sits down, he asks the gentleman sitting next to him, "Excuse me, is anyone sitting here?" The man says no.

Now, very excited to be in such a great seat for the game, Bob again inquires of the man next to him, "This is incredible! Who in their right mind would have a seat like this at the Superbowl and not use it?"

The man replies, "Well, actually, the seat belongs to me. I was supposed to come with my wife, but she passed away. This is the first Superbowl we haven't been to together since we got married in 1967."

"Well, that's really sad," says Bob. "But still, couldn't you find someone to take the seat? A relative or a close friend?"

"No," the man replies. "They're all at the funeral."

The player found out he'd been cut from the team when he came to the clubhouse and the attendant said, "No visitors."

☆ ☆ ☆

Poor grades were threatening to keep a star high school quarterback from playing in the conference championship game. His coach begged and pleaded with the school superintendent to let the boy play.

After much annoyance, the superintendent finally told the coach, "Bring your quarterback into my office. I'll give him a short quiz. If he passes, he can play. If not, you'll have to make do without him."

The coach went to get the player, and returned quickly. The superintendent asked the boy, "What is seven plus five?"

The quarterback thought for a moment, then answered, "Eleven."

The coach's face turned white. "Oh, give him another chance!" he pleaded. "He only missed it by two!"

☆ ☆ ☆

BASKETBALL THEOLOGY:

Three point shot: A sermon

Ejection: A crying child taken to the nursery

Slam dunk: A shorter than usual sermon

Free throw: A toddler tossing toys on the floor

Change of possession: The offering

Stewardship

One Monday morning, a minister was seen on a hilltop in the brisk wind flying a kite. "What are you doing, pastor?" someone asked.

"I'm just doing what I was told to do after the stewardship sermon yesterday," he answered.

✩ ✩ ✩

A youngster, in church for the first time, watched the ushers passing the offering plates. As they neared her pew, she whispered to her father, "Remember, Daddy, you don't have to pay for me. I'm under five."

✩ ✩ ✩

Jim, about five years old, was very restless as the sermon dragged on and on.

Finally he whispered to his father, "If we give him our money now, do you think he'll let us go?"

"I have always tithed," a man told his pastor, "but now I have a problem with tithing. When I began tithing, my weekly income was fifty dollars, and I gave five dollars to the church every Sunday. I was successful in business and my income rose to five hundred dollars a week, and I gave fifty dollars to the church every Sunday. Now my income is five thousand dollars a week, and I just can't bring myself to give five hundred dollars to my church every week."

"Why don't we pray over it?" the pastor said. He prayed, "Dear God, Please make this man's weekly income five hundred dollars a week so that he can tithe."

✧ ✧ ✧

When it comes to giving, some people stop at nothing.

✧ ✧ ✧

"Nothing inspires and strengthens my commitment like our stewardship campaign."

✧ ✧ ✧

During the service, the minister said, "My friends, we are in difficulty. We have some unexpected repair costs on our building. Any of you who can pledge one hundred dollars or more for this purpose, please stand up."

At that moment, the substitute organist played "The Star Spangled Banner."

Sunday School

A Sunday school teacher was having a hard time getting her young charges to grasp the message of the Good Samaritan. Finally she pointed to one of the children and asked, "Alison, suppose you passed a vacant lot and saw a man in ragged clothes lying on the ground, badly beaten up, covered with blood. What would you do?"

The eight-year-old said, "I think I would throw up."

☆ ☆ ☆

Sunday school teacher: "What became of Tyre?"
Pupil: "The Lord punctured it."

☆ ☆ ☆

A youngster asked his Sunday school teacher, "Do you think Noah did a lot of fishing when he was on the ark?"

The teacher said, "I imagine he did."

The kid asked, "With only two worms?"

393

"Can anyone name the Roman emperor who was most notorious for persecuting early Christians?" the Sunday school teacher asked.

"Nero," promptly responded one youth.

"That's right. What were some of the things he did?"

"He tortured the prisoners in Rome."

"And do you know how he tortured them?"

"He played the fiddle."

☆ ☆ ☆

A Sunday school teacher was discussing the Ten Commandments with her five- and six-year-olds. After explaining the commandment that teaches us to "honor thy father and thy mother," she asked, "Is there a commandment that teaches us how to treat our brothers and sisters?"

Without missing a beat, one little boy answered, "Thou shalt not kill."

☆ ☆ ☆

The Sunday school teacher had her children draw a picture of the manger scene for Christmas week. The students all drew wonderful variations on the same basic theme: Mary and Joseph, the Infant in the manger, the animals, the shepherds, the wise men. Something about little Wayne's drawing baffled her, though.

"What's that large box in front of everyone, with the lines coming out of the top?" she asked.

"That's their television set," Wayne said proudly.

The pastor visited a Sunday school class and later gave a report to the board about what he had found. He told them he had asked Johnnie, "Who knocked down the walls of Jericho?" and Johnnie had told him, "I didn't do it." When the pastor told Johnnie's teacher what Johnnie's answer was, the teacher had said, "If Johnnie said he didn't do it, Pastor, I'm sure he didn't do it."

"What do you think of that?" the minister asked the board. After some silent thought, a deacon spoke up and said, "Pastor, don't be too concerned. We have enough money in the bank to build a new one."

✩ ✩ ✩

The Sunday school teacher, wishing to point out the dangers of drink, dropped a worm into a glass of alcohol. The worm squirmed for a while and then died. "Now, what does that show you?" she asked. One boy came up with this answer, "If you drink alcohol, you'll never get worms."

✩ ✩ ✩

A father asked his son what he had learned in Sunday school:

"The Ten Commandments," the son replied.

"Did you understand them?" he was asked.

"All but one of them," he answered. "What does 'Thou shalt not commit agriculture' mean?"

"That means," his father explained, "Thou shalt not plough in thy neighbor's field."

Little Johnny came home from Sunday school bubbling with excitement. "And what did you learn today?" asked his father.

"Wow! What a story!" said Johnnie. "The teacher told us about Moses leading all the Israelites out of Egypt, with Pharoah's Egyptians chasing them. At the Red Sea, Moses dropped an atomic bomb! Bang! Pow! The waters of the Red Sea opened up, the Jews got across, the waters closed, and all the Egyptians were drowned."

"Tell me truthfully, Johnnie. Is that what your teacher told you?" gasped his father.

"Naw," said little Johnnie, "but, you'd never believe it if I told you the story the way he did."

☆　☆　☆

As they were on their way to the church service, a Sunday school teacher asked her little children, "And why is it necessary to be quiet in church?"

One bright little girl replied, "Because people are sleeping."

☆　☆　☆

After a lesson on heaven, a Sunday school teacher asked, "Where do you want to go?"

The class answered, "Heaven."

"That's good," she told them. "And what must we do to go to heaven?"

"Die."

A Sunday school teacher told her class about Good Friday, Maundy Thursday, Palm Sunday, and Easter. "This is holy week. Are there any questions?"

One boy raised his hand. "What happens if you don't want to be holy all week?"

✰ ✰ ✰

"Do you think there is a devil?" the Sunday school teacher asked her class.

One of the class said, "No, I think it's like Santa Claus. I know it's my daddy."

✰ ✰ ✰

A minister was explaining the wonders and beauty of heaven to a group of children. Then he asked, "How many of you want to go to heaven?" Every hand went up except one.

"Don't you want to go to heaven, Peter?" the minister asked.

"Yes, I do," Peter answered.

"Then why didn't you raise your hand?"

"I thought you were getting up a load to go now," Peter said.

✰ ✰ ✰

Casey approached her Sunday school teacher after class with a question: "If the people of Israel were Israelites and the people of Canaan were Canaanites, do we call the people living in Paris parasites?"

Tall Tales

William was notorious for stretching the truth outrageously. When he caught a fish, it quickly grew to three, five, eight, ten pounds, as he repeated the story. A slight accident became a near-death experience, in his words.

One day his minister sat down with him and warned him sternly of the dangers—both in this life and eternally—of constant lying. "When you feel the urge to embellish the facts," the clergyman suggested, tapping the cover of his Bible, "remember the Good Book."

The next day, William was telling friends about a stranger he'd just seen come out of the police station. "He had to have been 6 feet 10 inches. Fists the size of basketballs. Biceps like stovepipes. Mean-looking. I saw a glimmer of metal in the back of his car, and I'm sure it was a submachine gun."

William's minister had been standing nearby, unnoticed. He stepped forward and asked loudly, "And how much do you reckon this fellow weighed?"

William, dumbfounded, spotted the preacher's black Bible. "Er, I guess about ninety pounds."

Graham: "I hear your town weathered a terrible flood last week."

Bell: "Yeah, the mousetraps in our basement caught three fish."

☆ ☆ ☆

"The wind blows so hard on my farm in Kansas," a man said, "that if the hen is facing the wrong way, she lays the same egg five times."

☆ ☆ ☆

A Texan was picked up by a taxi at the Sydney airport. He started a tirade about how small the airport was, declaring that back in Texas there are bigger runways on ranches. As they crossed the Sydney harbor, he told the driver they had bigger duck ponds back home. In fact, the Texan had a disparaging comment to make about every feature they encountered on the drive to the hotel.

But the cab driver had the last word. When a kangaroo jumped in front of the cab, causing a sudden and severe stop, the driver said, "Stupid grasshopper."

Teenagers

A teenager came home after driving his dad's new car for the first time.

"I've got some good news and some bad news," he announced. "Which do you want to hear first."

"Let's start with the good news," his father replied.

"The good news is, the air bag works."

☆　☆　☆

"When Abraham Lincoln was your age," a man said to his lazy teenage son, "he was chopping wood, plowing fields, and hunting for food."

"When he was your age," the boy responded, "he was president of the United States."

☆　☆　☆

The best way to keep your teenagers at home is to make the home a pleasant place—and let the air out of their tires.

Somewhat skeptical of his son's newfound determination to become Charles Atlas, the father nevertheless followed the teenager over to the weight-lifting department.

"Please, Dad," wheedled the boy, "I promise I'll use 'em every day."

"I don't know, Michael. It's really a commitment on your part," the father pointed out.

"Please, Dad?"

"They're not cheap either."

"I'll use 'em Dad, I promise. You'll see."

Finally won over, the father paid for the equipment and headed for the door. From the corner of the store he heard his son yelp, "What? You mean I have to carry them to the car?"

☆ ☆ ☆

A sixteen-year-old boy and a fifteen-year-old girl wanted to get married. Both sets of parents objected strenuously, but the young couple was adamant. They loved each other and wanted to get married—and in a church. "If you won't let us," the girl insisted to her parents, "we'll just run away and get married."

Finally, it was agreed upon—a small ceremony in the church, attended only by the young couple and the four parents. The happy day arrived and the minister was performing the ceremony and the young groom was repeating his words after him:

Minister: "With all my worldly goods I thee endow."

Boy: "With all my worldly goods I thee endow."

Boy's mother (whispering to his father): "There goes his mountain bike."

401

The parents of a teenager got very tired of their daughter's bad attitude. "The trouble with you, Julie," said her mother, "is that all you do is grumble and complain."

"That's not true," snarled Julie. "I also gripe, crab, bellyache, carp, and grouse."

☆ ☆ ☆

A teenage girl who'd been talking on the phone for about a half-hour hung up just as her father walked by.

"Hey," he said, "that was short. You usually talk for two hours or more. What happened?"

"Wrong number," replied the girl.

☆ ☆ ☆

"What's the most difficult age to get a child to sleep regularly?" a new mother asked an older veteran of child rearing.

"About seventeen years."

☆ ☆ ☆

When your teenage children have friends in distant cities, you become much more concerned about obscene phone bills than you are about obscene phone calls.

☆ ☆ ☆

Kelly, sobbing: "I'm just devastated. No one has replied to my party invitations—and it's tonight!"
Dottie: "Well, if nobody wants to come, you can't stop them."

A young teenager was writing to her friend, listing the gifts she had received upon her graduation from junior high school. She wrote, ". . .and Grandma gave me a diary. It is a nice diary, but it's awfully late to start on a diary now. Everything has already happened."

Traffic Stops

A small town police officer stopped a motorist speeding down Main Street.

"But officer," the man began, "I can explain."

"Save it for later," snapped the officer. "I'm going to let you cool your heels in jail until the chief gets back."

"But, officer, I just wanted to say. . ."

"I said keep quiet! You're going to jail!" A few hours later the officer looked in on his prisoner and said, "Lucky for you, the chief's at his daughter's wedding. He'll be in a good mood when he gets back."

"Don't bet on it," answered the man in the cell. "I'm the groom."

✫ ✫ ✫

A police officer had discovered the perfect hiding place for nabbing speeders. On an average day, he would issue tickets to a dozen or more drivers. One day, however, everyone who passed was under the speed limit. The officer was baffled, but he soon discovered what was going on. About one hundred yards ahead of his hiding place, he found a ten-year-old boy standing by the side of the road with a huge hand-painted sign that read "RADAR TRAP AHEAD."

A little more investigative work led the officer to the sign-waver's accomplice, another boy, about one hundred yards beyond the radar trap, with a sign reading "TIPS" and a bucket full of change at his feet.

✫ ✫ ✫

The ABSOLUTE WORST things to say to a police officer:

"What can I do for you, Bucko?"

"Would you hold my beer while I get my license?"

"Sorry, Officer, I didn't realize my radar detector wasn't plugged in."

"Hey, you must've been doin' about 125 mph to keep up with me! Good job!"

"I was going to be a cop, but I decided to finish high school instead."

"Gee, that gut sure doesn't inspire confidence."

"Do you know why you pulled me over? Okay, just so one of us does."

"I was trying to keep up with traffic. Yes, I know there are no other cars around. That's how far ahead of me they are!"

Travel

"I just returned from Germany and had the most wonderful time," bubbled Ginger to her friends.

"I thought, before you left, you said you were having trouble with your German," Melody said.

"No, not at all. It was the Germans who had trouble with it."

☆ ☆ ☆

A man in a tour group thought he had mastered French well enough to speak for himself. With his guide standing by, he approached a couple of Parisians and struck up an eloquent conversation. The locals, however, didn't respond to his questions. At length, the villagers began conversing with each other in low voices.

"I give up," the tourist admitted to the guide. "What are they saying?"

"They're debating whether you were speaking English or German."

A guest at a second-class motel repeatedly rang the desk clerk late at night, each time to be placed on hold while the clerk juggled other calls. The guest would lose his patience with the permahold routine, hang up, and redial a few minutes later.

Finally, the clerk actually took his call—and didn't hesitate to express annoyance at the repeated rings. "This is about the fifth time you've rung me," the clerk began sternly. "You seem to have an incurable itch. What in the world is eating you?"

"Something in this carpet is, for sure," the guest agreed. "I think I have a right to know what it is."

☆ ☆ ☆

The college student was quite nervous on the first afternoon of his summer job as a resort hotel porter. A veteran at the bell desk gave him some friendly advice: "You'll get good tips if you chat with the guests and call them by name."

"Er, how do I find out their names? Do I sneak over to the reception desk before I take them to their room, or just come right out and ask them?"

"No, no. Neither. All you have to do is notice the name and address labels on their suitcases."

With this advice, the student porter escorted a well-dressed, elderly couple to their suite on the fourth floor. Reaching down to clutch a couple of bags, he slyly read the tag dangling off one of the handles.

"So," he ventured, "it's nice having you here, Mr. and Mrs. Leather. What brings you to the islands?"

An overweight businessman took his suitcase from the luggage ramp at the airport and huffed to the airline's courtesy desk. "What's the meaning of this?" he demanded, showing the agent the large, red-lettered handling tag tied to his suitcase handle.

The agent leaned over the counter and read the tag: FAT.

"I'm well aware of my weight problem," the businessman groused, "but what right does your airline have to comment on it in public?"

"Welcome to Fresno, sir," the ticket agent smiled. "FAT is the destination code for this airport."

☆　☆　☆

"How much will it cost me to fly to Dublin?" a man asked an airline ticket agent in Reno, Nevada.

After examining the database for different times and connections, the agent pointed out, "The lowest rates would involve long layovers in Denver and New York."

"Oh, it doesn't matter how long it takes. Just get me the lowest fare."

The agent punched a few more keys and came up with the reply: "Thirteen hundred and forty dollars, one way."

The man rubbed his chin. "That's still rather much, for me. What would it cost if I were to fly to New York and then connect with a train for the run over to Dublin?"

A man had driven all night, so when he passed a park in a small community, he decided to stop and take a nap. Just as he dozed off, there was a knock on the window.

The man saw a jogger at his window. The runner asked, "Excuse me, do you have the time?"

"Yeah, it's 6:12," the man replied and settled back to his nap. He was almost asleep again when there was another knock on the window.

Another jogger asked, "I'm sorry to disturb you. Do you have the time?"

"Yeah. It's 6:19." The man rolled up the window and decided he'd had enough of the questions, so he took paper and pen and made a sign reading: "I DON'T KNOW THE TIME." He stuck the sign in the window and again nestled himself back into the seat.

Before long, he heard another tap on his window. The man was annoyed to see another jogger, and he disgustedly rolled down the window and said, "Yeah, what is it?"

The jogger replied, "It's 6:26."

☆ ☆ ☆

A woman phoned a travel agent and demanded, "I need your finest accommodations in Ocala, Florida, for the week of the twentieth."

After a moment, the agent suggested, "I can book you a penthouse suite in the heart of town. First class in every respect."

"With a beachfront view, I assume."

"Er, no ma'am. Ocala isn't near the ocean."

"Don't give me that!" the woman snapped. "I've seen it on a map. Florida is a narrow state."

"Where did you go on your vacation?"

"Tahiti. It was gorgeous!"

"I'll bet! What did you do there?"

"Everything. We went snorkeling, ate wonderful island cuisine—but my most memorable experience was learning some of the tribal dances."

"Oooh, I'll bet that was interesting. How well did you do?"

"Well, the islanders gave me a special name after they saw me dance."

"What's your new name?"

"Awkward."

☆ ☆ ☆

Worn out from carrying the luggage and running for the train, the husband complained to his wife, "If you'd moved a little faster, we would have caught that train."

The wife retorted, "If you hadn't rushed, we wouldn't have had to wait so long for the next one!"

☆ ☆ ☆

"What kinds of papers do I need to travel to Europe?" a youth asked a travel agent.

"Basically, a passport and a visa."

"I have the passport, no problem. Do you think they'll accept MasterCard?"

A man walked into the railroad station of a small town and asked what time the train arrived. The agent said, "It comes in at eight P.M. and leaves at eight-fifteen."

Because it was only six o'clock, the man started to walk into town for a cup of coffee. When he was two blocks away from the station, he heard the whistle of an approaching train. He rushed back just as the train arrived and said angrily to the agent, "You told me the train came at eight! I could have missed it!"

The agent said, "Calm down, buster. That's yesterday's train!"

Virtues and Vices

"George Washington was born in Texas," a Texan proclaimed. "You see," he went on, "they lived out in West Texas where almost nothing grows. His father, however, did manage to get a little mesquite tree to grow in the front of the house. He watered it, tended to it, and took great pride in it. One day, when he got home from work, he found it had been chopped down.

" 'Now who did that?' George's father asked.

" 'Father,' George said, 'I chopped it down. I cannot tell a lie.'

" 'If you cannot tell a lie,' his father said, 'we cannot live in Texas.' And that is why they moved to Virginia."

☆ ☆ ☆

Mark Twain's wife tried to cure him of using foul language by using some of his own words. After a while, he told her, "Honey, you know the words, but you haven't got the tune."

"Joe," the minister said to one of his parishioners, "whiskey is your worst enemy."

"That may be," Joe answered, "but you told us to love our enemies."

"I know I did," the minister replied, "but I didn't tell you to swallow them."

✫　✫　✫

"I never met a man I didn't like," Will Rogers said.

"That's because," someone said, "he never met my brother-in-law."

✫　✫　✫

A truck driver who was being heckled by several members of a motorcycle gang at a diner walked out without responding to their taunts.

"Not much of a man," one of the bikers said to the waitress after the trucker had left.

With an amused smile, the waitress responded, "He's not much of a driver either. He just ran over a bunch of motorcycles out in the parking lot."

✫　✫　✫

Noel Coward wrote in his biography about his friendship with David Niven, who had the habit of biting his fingernails. From Paris, Coward sent him a postcard with a picture of Venus de Milo and a note saying, "See what will happen if you keep on biting your fingernails?"

The old cynic W. C. Fields said: "Smile first thing in the morning—and get it over with."

☆　☆　☆

A man stopped to help a woman with a flat tire on her car. As he started to raise the jack, she said to him, "Please do it as quietly as you can. My husband is asleep in the back seat."

Weather

The border between Russia and Poland was always being changed. One week the Russians held sway, the next week the countryside came under Polish control. But one thing was always certain. During the winter, the weather was awful.

Came a day when the Poles took over the territory. Podolski, one of the border sentries exclaimed, "Thank goodness! No more of those rotten Russian winters!"

✫ ✫ ✫

A man was driving home from an out-of-town trip and called his wife on the cellular phone. "I'll be home in about three hours," he observed. "I see the weather report calls for a twenty-percent chance of snow flurries there tonight."

"Well, be careful on the road," his wife said. "The children have been building twenty-percent snowmen and having twenty-percent snowball fights since lunchtime."

News Anchor: "So what's the chance of rain today?"
Meteorologist: "Oh, no worse than fifty percent."
Anchor: "And what's the chance you're wrong?"
Meteorologist: "About the same."

☆　☆　☆

A minister is often looked upon to exert influence for good weather or take responsibility for bad weather. He then has to remind people that he is in sales and not in management.

☆　☆　☆

"How did you find the weather in London?" asked a man's wife upon his return from a long trip.

"You don't have to find the weather in London," he replied. "It bumps into you at every corner."

☆　☆　☆

After months of discouraging failures in his daily weather forecasts, a TV meteorologist submitted his resignation.

"But you have such a friendly screen presence," the station manager protested. "Our audiences love you, even when you get the forecasts wrong."

"Thanks, but I really think I need to be in a different locale altogether."

"Why?"

"Well, it's obvious that the weather here just doesn't agree with me."

The little girl walked to and from school every day. One morning, though, the weather was questionable and clouds were forming. She still made her daily trek to the elementary school, but as the day progressed, the winds whipped up along with thunder and lightning. The girl's mother became concerned that her daughter would be frightened as she walked home from school, and she feared that the electrical storm might harm her child. So the mother quickly got into her car and drove along the route to her daughter's school.

Finally, up ahead, she saw her little girl walking along, but with each flash of lightning, the child would stop, look up at the sky, and smile. This happened two or three times while the mother watched. Lightning would flash, and the girl would stop and smile.

When she had pulled the car alongside her daughter, the mother called her over to the car and asked, "What are you doing?"

The girl answered, "I'm just walking home, but God keeps taking pictures of me."

☆   ☆   ☆

Some Indians asked the medicine man what kind of winter they might expect so they would know how much wood to chop. Just to be sure they would chop enough, he told them it would be severe. They went out and did a lot of chopping but got tired of all the hard work and came back and asked, "Are you sure we're going to have a hard winter?"

To keep the chopping going he said, "Yes, it's

probably going to be even worse than I predicted." They went back to their chopping.

Soon the medicine man began to feel guilty about putting all this extra work on them, so he called the local weather station and asked them about the coming winter. He was told it would indeed be a difficult winter. "Are you sure?" he asked.

"Oh, yes," the meteorologist told him, "we're absolutely sure about this. You see, the Indians know about things like this and they're chopping wood like crazy."

Weddings

A nervous groom stood in front of the minister. He was perspiring, his knees wobbled, he looked wretched. Ignoring the young man's plight, the minister began guiding the couple through their vows:

"Wilt thou. . .love. . .cherish. . .care for. . .and so on?" he intoned.

"I wilt," the young man replied.

☆ ☆ ☆

A little boy was in his sister's wedding. As he was going down the aisle, he would take two steps, stop and turn to the crowd, alternating between the bride's side and the groom's side. While facing the crowd, he would put his hands up like claws and roar. So it went step, step, claw, roar, all the way down the aisle. The crowd was in tears from laughing.

When asked what he was doing, he replied, "I was being the ring bear."

A pastor received this note from a person he had married: "Dear Pastor: I appreciated the marriage ceremony you performed. It was wonderful the way you brought my happiness to a conclusion."

☆ ☆ ☆

A minister sought to dispel the bride's nervousness by telling her to concentrate on familiar objects during her walk down the aisle. "First," he told her, "think about the aisle, which you've walked down so often. Then focus on the altar with the pretty flowers. Finally, think of George—he'll be there, waiting for you with a smile on his face."

On the day of the wedding, the congregation was surprised to hear the bride coming down the aisle muttering audibly: "Aisle, Altar, George. I'll alter George."

☆ ☆ ☆

"Let me ask you a few questions," a minister said to an old man in a nursing home who wanted to get married.

"Do you love her?"

"No."

"Is she a Christian?"

"I don't know."

"Does she have a lot of money?"

"I don't think so."

"Then why are you marrying her?"

"She can drive at night."

A groom was asked if he was entering the marriage of his own free will. After looking at his bride, he answered, "Put down 'yes.' "

Wit and Wisdom

Skip: "Stupid people are always sure of themselves.
Smart people question everything."
Rip: "Are you sure about that?"

☆ ☆ ☆

When antique dealers get together, how do they
strike up a conversation? Does one of them venture,
"What's new?"

☆ ☆ ☆

Necessity is the mother of invention—even though
much of what's invented is hardly necessary.

☆ ☆ ☆

A lot of government policies make about as much sense
as interstate highways in Hawaii.

Has anyone noticed that it now costs more to entertain the average teenager than it cost both parents to get through college?

☆　☆　☆

The primary difference between wives and husbands is that the wives never forget special occasions and the husbands never remember.

☆　☆　☆

A good sermon is one that goes in one ear and out the other—and smacks somebody else right between the eyes.

☆　☆　☆

Grandpa: "Lincoln was right when he said, 'You can fool all the people some of the time and some of the people all the time.'"
Grandson: "But what happens the rest of the time?"
Grandpa: "They're likely to make fools of themselves, I reckon."

☆　☆　☆

"As your grandpa always said, 'If it ain't broke, don't fix it,'" the father told his son, a college engineering student.
　　"As my professor always says, 'If it ain't broke, it doesn't have enough features,'" parried the student.

Abraham Lincoln remarked that common folks are the best in the country. "That is the reason the Lord made so many of them."

☆　☆　☆

There's no such thing as a beautiful newborn baby— until you become a parent.

☆　☆　☆

Why is it you can buy cigarettes at a gas station—where smoking is strictly forbidden?

☆　☆　☆

It's better to say nothing and have people wonder about your intelligence than to speak and remove all doubt.

☆　☆　☆

If it goes without saying. . .then let it go without saying.

☆　☆　☆

It's a sad fact that fifty percent of marriages end in divorce. The other half end in death. You could be one of the lucky ones.

☆　☆　☆

When my critics stop hissing, I know I'm slipping.

How can time be such a wonderful healer—but such a terrible beautician?

☆ ☆ ☆

He hasn't an enemy in the world—but all his friends hate him.

☆ ☆ ☆

When a man brings his wife flowers for no reason, there's a reason.

☆ ☆ ☆

All marriages are happy. It's trying to live together that causes all the problems.

☆ ☆ ☆

Marriage means commitment. Of course, so does insanity.

☆ ☆ ☆

I had some words with my wife, and she had some paragraphs with me.

☆ ☆ ☆

He had a magnificent build before his stomach went in for a career of its own.

"Now, Bruno," the teacher said to the aggressive youngster, "what do you think your classmates would think if you were always kind and polite?"

"They'd think they could beat me up," responded the kid promptly.

☆ ☆ ☆

Grandma: "You should pay attention and try to learn from the mistakes of others."
Granddaughter: "Why?"
Grandma: "Well, nobody's ever lived long enough to make all the mistakes themselves."

☆ ☆ ☆

A Boston native was asked why she didn't travel. "Why should I?" she asked. "I'm already here."

☆ ☆ ☆

Wallace: "You sure look glum. What's wrong? I thought you said last week that everything seemed to be coming your way."
Alice: "Yeah. I think I was on a one-way street, headed in the wrong direction."

☆ ☆ ☆

Jokes and history are the same—they repeat themselves.

The wages of sin is alimony.

☆　☆　☆

Love may be blind, but marriage is a real eye opener.

☆　☆　☆

A woman was vacationing in Sante Fe. On the veranda of the Old State Building, Indians sell handmade jewelry. She noticed a necklace made from curious-looking teeth and asked the old Indian, "What are those?"

"Those are grizzly bear teeth," he explained.

"Ah, yes," she replied, "and I suppose they have the same value for you that a string of pearls would have for me."

"Not exactly," he replied. "Anybody can open an oyster."

☆　☆　☆

My philosophy is, I only dread one day at a time.

☆　☆　☆

Gambling is a sure way of getting nothing for something.

☆　☆　☆

Opportunity knocks once. Difficulty never stops knocking.

If ignorance is bliss, why aren't more people happy?

✫ ✫ ✫

It will be interesting to see how long the meek can keep the earth after they inherit it.

✫ ✫ ✫

We probably wouldn't worry what people thought of us if we knew how seldom they do.

Work

"What do you mean I'm not qualified?" demanded a job applicant. "I have an IQ of 150. I scored 1,480 on the SAT. I was magna cum laude in graduate school."

"Yes," replied the hiring supervisor, "but we don't really require intelligence around here."

☆ ☆ ☆

"Tell me, Mrs. Harris, have you any other skills you think might be worth mentioning?" the interviewer asked.

"Actually, yes," she said. "Last year I had two short stories published in national magazines, and I finished a novel."

"Very impressive, but I was thinking of skills you could apply during office hours."

The applicant explained brightly, "Oh, that was during office hours."

A recent job applicant wrote: "I graduated first in my class at Harvard. Last year I refused to accept a vice-presidency at GM. I don't care what salary I'm offered because money has no meaning to me. I never look at the clock and will work eighty hours a week if I have to."

After examining the application, the personnel manager said, "Don't you have even one weak spot?"

The applicant said, "They say I fib a little."

☆ ☆ ☆

A boss tried to help one of his employees improve his ways by telling him, "You have one bad habit. You never listen when people are talking to you. You get a faraway look and your mind wanders off. Promise me you'll work on that."

The employee responded, "What was that you were saying?"

☆ ☆ ☆

Boss: "This office looks as though it hasn't been cleaned for a month."

Maid: "That's not my fault. I only started work Monday."

☆ ☆ ☆

Boss: "Why are you always late getting to work?"

Employee: "Well, it's been my experience that it helps make the day go by quicker."

"Why don't you apply for a job where I work?" Dick asked an out-of-work buddy. "They're hiring."

"How long are the hours?"

"Sixty minutes, same as every place else."

☆ ☆ ☆

First Manager: Say what happened to all those "Think" signs you used to have posted on the walls?

Second Manager: I had to take 'em down. Everyone was sitting around thinking and no work was getting done.

☆ ☆ ☆

"What special skills do you have?" a company official asked a job applicant.

"Well, none, actually," admitted the applicant.

"I'm afraid we can't use you, then. We have several unskilled positions, but they're all filled right now by the president's relatives."

☆ ☆ ☆

The boss said, "What's this I hear about your going to church and praying for a raise? Don't ever go over my head again!"

☆ ☆ ☆

"My cousin works for the IRS," said Edward.

"Who doesn't?" replied Fran.

A dynamite explosion at a road construction site sent old Bill flying into oblivion. A few minutes later, the foreman came around to find out what had happened.

"Where's old Bill?" he asked.

"He left," said a coworker.

"When did he say he'd be back?"

"He didn't say. But if he comes back as quick as he left, I'd say he'll be back about five minutes ago."

☆ ☆ ☆

The company's management team put their heads together to decide how to reduce the high employee turnover rate.

"They spend their first six or eight weeks learning our system, then they join another company," complained one executive.

"Yes, but doesn't that at least speak highly of our training program?" chirped an optimistic colleague.

☆ ☆ ☆

A sawmill worker dropped a quarter, bent over to pick it up and accidentally got an ear cut off by the circular blade. His hollering drew a crowd of coworkers. Together, they started searching the sawdust for his severed ear.

After a minute, one of the searchers came up with an ear and handed it to the injured man. He examined it carefully, then tossed it away. "That ain't it," he said, resuming his probe. "My ear had a fountain pen behind it."

You can always tell a good office manager. He's got that worried look on his assistant's face!

✫   ✫   ✫

Andy wanted a job as a signalman on the railways and was told to meet the inspector at the signal box.

The inspector put this question to him: "What would you do if you realized that two trains were heading for each other on the same track?"

Andy said, "I would switch the points for one of the trains."

"What if the lever broke?" asked the inspector.

"Then I'd dash down out of the signal box," said Andy, "and I'd use the manual lever over there."

"What if that had been struck by lightning?"

"Then," Andy continued, "I'd run back into the signal box and phone the next signal box."

"What if the phone was busy?"

"Well, in that case, "persevered Andy, "I'd rush down and use the public emergency phone along the track."

"What if that was vandalized?"

"Oh, well, then I'd run into the village and get my uncle Silas."

This puzzled the inspector, so he asked, "Why would you do that?"

"Because," Andy replied, "he's never seen a train crash."

✫   ✫   ✫

Where he worked, he had four hundred people under him. He was a guard in a cemetery.

Job Interviewer: "What do you consider your greatest weakness?"
Applicant: "I'm a workaholic."

✫ ✫ ✫

Job Interviewer: "What were your three strongest subjects in college?"
Applicant: "Italian, German, and trigonometry."
Interviewer: "Let me hear you say 'good day' in Italian."
Applicant: "Buon giorno."
Interviewer: "And in German. . .?"
Applicant: "Guten tag."
Interviewer: "And in trigonometry. . .?"

✫ ✫ ✫

The only man who ever got his work done by Friday was Robinson Crusoe!

✫ ✫ ✫

Al was finding it difficult to sleep at night. He begged his doctor to give him a strong sedative. The doctor obliged, but told him to take only half of the prescribed pill. To make sure he slept, Al took a whole pill and went to sleep.

Al awoke to a warm, sunny dawn. He felt refreshed and cheerful. As he walked into the office, he saw his boss and said, "I'm ready. I slept like a log. I jumped out of bed like a kid this morning."

The boss said, "Nice. But where were you yesterday?"

"And what does your son do?" asked Mrs. Roper.

"Oh, he chose to follow the medical profession," said Mrs. Green.

"Wonderful! Is he a surgeon?"

"Actually, he's an undertaker."

☆ ☆ ☆

A corporate coach was lecturing a class of new management personnel. Positive thinking was the theme, and it was pounded home with example after example from the "real world." The coach was so confident of his message that he concluded, "As you can see, there's absolutely nothing that can't be accomplished with planning and delegation."

He then called for questions.

Only one young associate ventured to raise a hand. "Are you saying our company could find a way to get toothpaste back in the tube?"

☆ ☆ ☆

"Good news and bad news," reported an employee representative returning to the job after a weekly meeting with management.

"Give us the bad news first," mumbled a colleague.

"They're canceling the company's fire insurance policy."

"And the good news?"

"They're buying us a fire truck."

Job applicant: "Why won't you hire me? I have a record
of success and years of experience."
Personnel director: "Yes, but it's all in sales. This job
requires management skills."
Applicant: "Sales, management—same basic principles."
Director: "Yeah. Forest fires, bombs—why not station
Smokey the Bear at O'Hare International Airport?"

☆ ☆ ☆

A secretary said to a co-worker, "I finally got my boss to
laugh out loud."
"Did you tell him a joke?"
"No, I asked for raise!"

☆ ☆ ☆

The secretary entered a crowded elevator at the end of the
day, headed for home. Without thinking, she pressed
the ground floor button twice in rapid succession.
Another secretary noticed and commented knowingly, "You must keep your hand on a computer mouse
all day, too."

☆ ☆ ☆

An elderly man came into an office and asked the manager, "Can I see Eddie Carson? I'm his grandfather."
"He's not here," the manager replied. "He's at your
funeral!"

A man was commiserating to his wife about his job. "They expect us to make every second count," he griped, "but they force us to do things that waste time."

"What kinds of things?"

"Like, we're required to check the bulletin board at least three times a day. I have to walk all the way to the other end of the plant. Takes a full five minutes every trip."

"But aren't the notices important?"

"Well, there was a posting this morning titled New Personal Injury Policy. The message said, 'A memo concerning this topic will be forthcoming later today.'"

☆　☆　☆

A supervisor happened into the break room and saw four of his staff sitting around a table. One was reading a magazine. The other three were waving imaginary rifles, shouting, "Pow! Pow! Pow!"

"What in the world's going on?" the boss demanded.

"We're holed up at Fort Dodge," one of the pantomimers replied, breathless. "We're being attacked by outlaws, and we're about to run out of ammunition."

The supervisor shook his head. "I think you've had too much break time." Turning to the quiet reader, he said, "Do me a favor. See that they all stop the nonsense and get back to work."

The fourth worker put down the magazine and shouted, "We gotta hit the trail, podners!" He flicked his wrists in front of him. "Giddyap!"

"I need a progress report concerning the Dempsey file," an executive told the assistant.

"Can I get it to you tomorrow?"

The executive raised an eyebrow. "If I wanted it tomorrow, that's the day I would have asked."

☆　☆　☆

Boss: "Why are you sitting around loafing?"

Worker: "Sorry. I didn't realize you were here."

Writers

Writing is easy. All you have to do is put a blank piece of paper in the typewriter, and put down what occurs to you. It's the occurring that's hard.

☆ ☆ ☆

During a dinner party at a small Montmartre cafe, Ernest Hemingway was boring the other diners with a long story about Pamplona, a story he'd told a dozen times before. Seated against the wall, Gertrude Stein said, "My dear, my leg has fallen asleep. Do you mind if I join it?"

☆ ☆ ☆

Mark Twain said he once spent a morning writing with the following result. He started by putting "The" on his paper. He stared at this for a long time. After several hours he added, "heck with it" and went fishing.

"How are you getting on with your magazine writing?"

"I'm holding my own. They send me back as much as I send them!"

☆ ☆ ☆

A reporter visited Hannibal, Missouri, to find out how Samuel Clemens (Mark Twain) had become such a good writer. He talked with a man who'd grown up with Clemens, who explained the secret of the writer's great success. "Shucks," he said, "I knew all those stories Sam told. He just wrote them down."

☆ ☆ ☆

An author sat in a department store autographing copies of his new book. He was especially pleased when one man brought up not only the new book, but several of his previous novels, saying, "My wife really likes your writing, so I've decided to give her these for her birthday."

"Oh, a surprise?" the author asked.

"I'll say," the customer agreed. "She's expecting a Cadillac."

About Bern Brunsting

Bernard Brunsting is a retired pilot and minister. During World War II he was a pilot of a B-17 bomber with a crew of ten, flying combat missions in the European Theater. After a time with an airline he entered seminary.

He has had thirteen books published, including a religious best-seller. His sermons have been published with those of Norman Vincent Peale in *Plus Magazine*, sent to more than one million subscribers each month.

During vacation periods, Bern has served English-speaking churches in all parts of the world, and for two summers was chaplain for the British and American embassies in Moscow. He has also served as chaplain for a number of around-the-world cruises on the Holland American Line.

Bern's hobbies include golf, travel, reading, and writing. He and his wife have been married for fifty-eight years.

Heard a Good Joke Lately? Jot it Down!

_____

_____

_____

_____

_____

_____

_____

_____

_____

_____

_____

_____

_____

_____

Heard a Good Joke Lately? Jot it Down!

_____

_____

_____

_____

_____

_____

_____

_____

_____

_____

_____

_____

_____

_____

_____

Heard a Good Joke Lately? Jot it Down!

_____

_____

_____

_____

_____

_____

_____

_____

_____

_____

_____

_____

_____

_____

_____

_____

Heard a Good Joke Lately? Jot it Down!

_____

_____

_____

_____

_____

_____

_____

_____

_____

_____

_____

_____

_____

_____

_____

Heard a Good Joke Lately? Jot it Down!

_____

_____

_____

_____

_____

_____

_____

_____

_____

_____

_____

_____

_____

LIKE JOKES OR TRIVIA?

Then check out these great books from
Barbour Publishing!

*A Funny Thing Happened on My Way Through the
Bible* by Brad Densmore
> A different twist on the traditional Bible trivia
> book. Share it with family and friends!
> Paperback. $2.49

*500 Clean Jokes and Humorous Stories and How to
Tell Them* by Rusty Wright and Linda Raney Wright
> Everything you need to improve your "humor
> quotient"—all from a Christian perspective.
> Paperback. $2.49

Fun Facts about the Bible by Robyn Martins
> Challenging and intriguing Bible trivia—expect
> some of the answers to surprise you!
> Paperback. $2.49

Available wherever books are sold.
Or order from:

Barbour Publishing, Inc.
P.O. Box 719
Uhrichsville, OH 44683
http://www.barbourbooks.com

If you order by mail add $2.00 to your order for shipping.
Prices subject to change without notice.